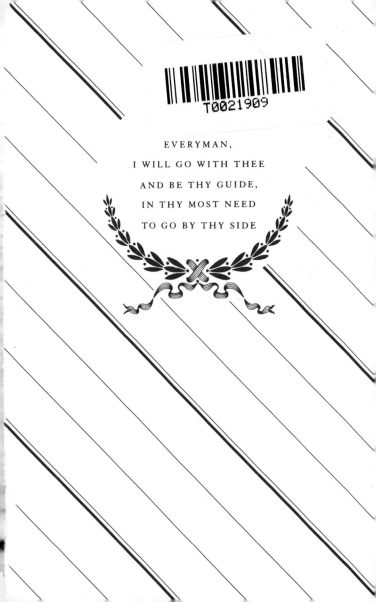

EVERYMAN,
I WILL GO WITH THEE
AND BE THY GUIDE,
IN THY MOST NEED
TO GO BY THY SIDE

EVERYMAN'S LIBRARY
POCKET POETS

DAY AND NIGHT

DIVERSIONS

POEMS OF LONDON

EDITED BY
CHRISTOPHER REID

EVERYMAN'S LIBRARY
POCKET POETS

Alfred A. Knopf New York London Toronto

THIS IS A BORZOI BOOK
PUBLISHED BY ALFRED A. KNOPF

This selection by Christopher Reid
first published in Everyman's Library, 2021
Copyright © 2021 by Everyman's Library

A list of acknowledgments to copyright owners appears
at the back of this volume.

All rights reserved. Published in the United States by Alfred A.
Knopf, a division of Penguin Random House LLC, New York, and
in Canada by Penguin Random House Canada Limited, Toronto.
Distributed by Penguin Random House LLC, New York. Published
in the United Kingdom by Everyman's Library, 50 Albemarle
Street, London W1S 4BD and distributed by Penguin Random
House UK, 20 Vauxhall Bridge Road, London SW1V 2SA.

www.randomhouse/everymans
www.everymanslibrary.co.uk

ISBN 978-0-593-32020-4 (US)
978-1-84159-824-6 (UK)

A CIP catalogue record for this book is available
from the British Library

Typography by Peter B. Willberg

Typeset in the UK by Input Data Services Ltd, Isle Abbotts, Somerset

Printed and bound in Germany
by GGP Media GmbH, Pössneck

CONTENTS

THE CITY AND WESTMINSTER

9

NATURE AND PLACE

SOME LONDONERS

FOREWORD

Whether you live in London, as I have done for almost
fifty years, or are on a brief visit, you cannot help being
reminded of both the geographical extent and the his-
torical depth of the city. How do you make sense of
it all?

For the purposes of this anthology – a pocket-size
book about a vast and teeming place – I have begun at
the centre. Think of the River Thames as the artery
that from earliest days has allowed London's heart, the
City of London, to beat. There and in Westminster is
where you will find the greatest concentration of the
traces of history, some well-preserved and plain to
see, others more hidden. But there is no need to rely
just on old buildings and monuments: poets from the
Early Modern period onward have been among the
busiest and liveliest chroniclers, whether reporting
events or imagining them, celebrating metropolitan
life or deploring it; and while the evidence they offer
is necessarily partial, it adds up to a considerable body
of witness.

William Blake stands on a different plane from his
fellows in having attempted, single-handed, something
more ambitious: the articulation, in his prophetic books
Milton and *Jerusalem*, of a comprehensive mythology
of London. Blake may still be thought eccentric, as he

was in his own day, but his is the spirit that I have come to regard as presiding over my choice of poems, extracts from poems, song lyrics, topical doggerel and poetically charged prose. Embracing not only the city centre, but also the districts and boroughs that sprawl around and away from it, Blake's vision strikes me as a vigorous assertion of eccentricity as the most reliable means of seeing the place as it really is.

So the following pages set out, in their own manner, to do justice to the full range between history and mythology, objective reality and the private feelings of the individual. The past – some of it proud, much disgraceful – looms large; but London's habit of growing and changing needs to be considered as well. With this in mind, I have placed in my final section a handful of poems addressing the experiences of immigrants who have become citizens. Regrettably, it has not been possible to include a section about London as the revitalizing new intake of the future will know it.

I should like to thank Charles Boyle, Eleanor Bron, Nancy Campbell, Neil Corcoran, Tom Deveson, Cliff Forshaw, Vivi Lachs, Alan Leith, Lord Lisvane and Gwyneth Powell for their advice and assistance with this book.

Christopher Reid

THE THAMES AND
OTHER WATERWAYS

THE RIVER'S TALE
(*Prehistoric*)

Twenty bridges from Tower to Kew –
(Twenty bridges or twenty-two) –
Wanted to know what the River knew,
For they were young, and the Thames was old,
And this is the tale that River told: –

'I walk my beat before London Town,
Five hours up and seven down.
Up I go till I end my run
At Tide-end-town, which is Teddington.
Down I come with the mud in my hands
And plaster it over the Maplin Sands.
But I'd have you know that these waters of mine
Were once a branch of the River Rhine,
When hundreds of miles to the East I went
And England was joined to the Continent.

'I remember the bat-winged lizard-birds,
The Age of Ice and the mammoth herds,
And the giant tigers that stalked them down
Through Regent's Park into Camden Town.
And I remember like yesterday
The earliest Cockney who came my way,

When he pushed through the forest that lined
    the Strand,
With paint on his face and a club in his hand.
He was death to feather and fin and fur.
He trapped my beavers at Westminster.
He netted my salmon, he hunted my deer,
He killed my heron off Lambeth Pier.
He fought his neighbour with axes and swords,
Flint or bronze, at my upper fords,
While down at Greenwich, for slaves and tin,
The tall Phoenician ships stole in,
And North Sea war-boats, painted and gay,
Flashed like dragon-flies, Erith way;
And Norseman and Negro and Gaul and Greek
Drank with the Britons in Barking Creek,
And life was gay, and the world was new,
And I was a mile across at Kew!
But the Roman came with a heavy hand,
And bridged and roaded and ruled the land,
And the Roman left and the Danes blew in –
And that's where your history-books begin!'

From POLY-OLBION

But now this mighty flood, upon his voyage prest
(That found how with his strength his beauties still
    increased,
From where brave Windsor stood on tiptoe to behold
The fair and goodly Thames, so far as ere he could,
With kingly houses crowned, of more than earthly
    pride,
Upon his either banks, as he along doth glide)
With wonderful delight doth his long course pursue,
Where Oatlands, Hampton Court, and Richmond he
    doth view,
Then Westminster the next great Thames doth
    entertain;
That vaunts her palace large, and her most sumptuous
    fane:
The land's tribunal seat that challengeth for hers,
The crowning of our kings, their famous sepulchres.
Then goes he on along by that more beauteous
    strand,
Expressing both the wealth and bravery of the land.
(So many sumptuous bowers within so little space
The all-beholding sun scarce sees in all his race.)
And on by London leads, which like a crescent lies,
Whose windows seem to mock the star-befreckled
    skies;

Besides her rising spires, so thick themselves that
    show,
As do the bristling reeds within his banks that grow.
There sees his crowded wharfs, and people-pestered
    shores,
His bosom overspread with shoals of labouring oars:
With that most costly bridge that doth him most
    renown,
By which he clearly puts all other rivers down.

IMPRESSION DU MATIN

The Thames nocturne of blue and gold
    Changed to a Harmony in grey:
    A barge with ochre-coloured hay
Dropped from the wharf: and chill and cold

The yellow fog came creeping down
    The bridges, till the houses' walls
    Seemed changed to shadows, and St. Paul's
Loomed like a bubble o'er the town.

Then suddenly arose the clang
    Of waking life; the streets were stirred
    With country waggons: and a bird
Flew to the glistening roofs and sang.

But one pale woman all alone,
    The daylight kissing her wan hair,
    Loitered beneath the gas lamps' flare,
With lips of flame and heart of stone.

OSCAR WILDE (1854–1900)

From THE HORSE'S MOUTH

I was walking by the Thames. Half-past morning on
an autumn day. Sun in a mist. Like an orange in a fried
fish shop. All bright below. Low tide, dusty water and a
crooked bar of straw, chicken-boxes, dirt and oil from
mud to mud. Like a viper swimming in skim milk. The
old serpent, symbol of nature and love.

> Five windows light the caverned man; through one he
>   breathes the air
> Through one hears music of the spheres; through one
>   can look
> And see small portions of the eternal world.

Such as Thames mud turned into a bank of nine
carat gold rough from the fire. They say a chap just out
of prison runs into the nearest cover; into some dark
little room, like a rabbit put up by a stoat. The sky feels
too big for him. But I liked it. I swam in it. I couldn't
take my eyes off the clouds, the water, the mud. And
I must have been hopping up and down Greenbank
Hard for half an hour grinning like a gargoyle, until
the wind began to get up my trousers and down my
back, and to bring me to myself, as they say. Meaning
my liver and lights.

And I perceived that I hadn't time to waste on pleas-
ure. A man of my age has to get on with the job.

I had two and six left from my prison money. I reck-
oned that five pounds would set me up with bed, board
and working capital. That left four pounds seventeen
and six to be won. From friends. But when I went over
my friends, I seemed to owe them more than that; more
than they could afford.

The sun had crackled into flames at the top; the mist
was getting thin in places, you could see crooked lines
of grey, like old cracks under spring ice. Tide on the
turn. Snake broken up. Emeralds and sapphires. Water
like varnish with bits of gold leaf floating thick and
heavy. Gold is the metal of intellect. And all at once the
sun burned through in a new place, at the side, and shot
out a ray that hit the Eagle and Child, next the motor
boat factory, right on the new signboard.

A sign, I thought. [. .]

COMPOSED UPON WESTMINSTER BRIDGE, SEPTEMBER 3, 1802

Earth has not anything to show more fair:
Dull would he be of soul who could pass by
A sight so touching in its majesty:
The City now doth, like a garment, wear
The beauty of the morning: silent, bare,
Ships, towers, domes, theatres, and temples lie
Open unto the fields, and to the sky;
All bright and glittering in the smokeless air.
Never did sun more beautifully steep
In his first splendour, valley, rock, or hill;
Ne'er saw I, never felt, a calm so deep!
The river glideth at his own sweet will:
Dear God! the very houses seem asleep;
And all that mighty heart is lying still.

COMPOSED UNDERNEATH
WESTMINSTER BRIDGE

Broad gravel barges shove the drift. Each wake
Thwacks the stone steps. A rearing tugboat streaked
Pass moorhens dabbing floss, spun pinkish-beaked.
Peanuts in caramelised burnt chocolate bake
Through syrupy air. Above, fried onions cake.
Pigeons on steel-eyed dates neck-wrestled, piqued,
Oblivious to their squabs that whined and squeaked
In iron-ringed nests, nursed on high struts. Opaque
Brown particles swarm churning through the tide.
That navy hoop of cormorant can compose
A counter to this shield – eagles splayed wide,
Gold martlets – on the bridge's side; it glows
While through the eau-de-nil flaked arches slide
The boats 'Bert Prior' and 'The Eleanor Rose'.

TOWN IN 1917

London
Used to wear her lights splendidly,
Flinging her shawl-fringe over the River,
Tassels in abandon.

And up in the sky
A two-eyed clock, like an owl
Solemnly used to approve, chime, chiming
Approval, goggle-eyed fowl!

There are no gleams on the River,
No goggling clock;
No sound from St. Stephen's;
No lamp-fringed frock.

Instead
Darkness, and skin-wrapped
Fleet, hurrying limbs,
Soft-footed dead.

London
Original, wolf-wrapped
In pelts of wolves, all her luminous
Garments gone.

London, with hair
Like a forest darkness, like a marsh
Of rushes, ere the Romans
Broke in her lair.

It is well
That London, lair of sudden
Male and female darknesses
Has broken her spell.

D. H. LAWRENCE (1885–1930)

FROST FAIR 1684

Behold the Wonder of this present Age,
A Famous RIVER now become a Stage.
Question not what I now declare to you,
The Thames is now both Fair and Market too.
And many Thousands daily do resort
There to behold the Pastime and the Sport.
Early and late, used by young and old
And valu'd not the fierceness of the cold
And did not think of that Almighty Hand
Who made the Waters bare, like to the Land:
Thousands and Thousand to the River flocks
Where mighty flakes of Ice do lye like Rocks.
There may you see the Coaches swiftly run,
As if beneath the ice were Waters none.
And sholes of People every where there be
Just like to Herrings in the brackish Sea;
And there the quaking Water-men will stand ye,
Kind Master, drink you beer, or Ale, or Brandy:
Walk in kind Sir, this Booth it is the chief,
We'l entertain you with a slice of Beef,
And what you please to Eat or Drink, 'tis here
No Booth, like mine, affords such dainty cheer.
Another crys, Here Master, they but scoff ye,
Here is a Dish of famous new-made Coffee.
And, some do say, a giddy senseless Ass

May on the THAMES be furnished with a Lass.
But to be short, such Wonders there are seen,
That in this Age before hath never been.
[. .]
There on a Sign you may most plainly see't,
Here's the first Tavern built in Freezeland-street:
There is Bull-baiting and Bear-baiting too,
That no man living yet e're found so true;
And Foot-Ball play is there so common grown,
That on the Thames before was never known;
Coals being dear, are carry'd on Mens backs,
And some on Sledges there are drawn in Sacks;
Men do on Horse-back ride from shore to shore,
Which formerly in Boats were wafted o're:
Poor people hard shifts make for livelihoods,
And happy are if they can sell their Goods;
What you can buy for Three-pence on the shore,
Will cost you Four-pence on the Thames, or more.
Now let me come to things more strange, yet true,
And question not what I declare to you;
There Roasted was a great and well-fed Oxe,
And there, with Dogs, Hunted the cunning Fox;
Dancing o'th' Ropes, and Puppit-plays likewise,
The like before ne'r seen beneath the Skies;
All stand admir'd, and very well they may.
To see such pastimes, and such sorts of play.

ANONYMOUS BROADSHEET (1684)   29

From AN ARRANT THIEF

All sorts of men work all the means they can,
To make a Thief of every waterman:
And as it were in one consent they join,
To trot by land i' th' dirt, and save their coin.
Carroaches, coaches, jades, and Flanders mares,
Do rob us of our shares, our wares, our fares:
Against the ground, we stand and knock our heels,
Whilst all our profit runs away on wheels;
And, whosoever but observes and notes,
The great increase of coaches and of boats,
Shall find their number more than e'er they were,
By half and more, within these thirty years.
Then watermen at sea had service still,
And those that staid at home had work at will:
Then upstart Hell-cart-coaches were to seek,
A man could scarce see twenty in a week;
But now I think a man may daily see,
More than the wherrys on the Thames can be.
When Queen Elizabeth came to the crown,
A coach in England then was scarcely known,
Then 'twas as rare to see one, as to spy
A Tradesman that had never told a lie.

CHARON

The conductor's hands were black with money:
Hold on to your ticket, he said, the inspector's
Mind is black with suspicion, and hold on to
That dissolving map. We moved through London,
We could see the pigeons through the glass but failed
To hear their rumour of wars, we could see
The lost dog barking but never knew
That his bark was as shrill as a cock crowing,
We just jogged on, at each request
Stop there was a crowd of aggressively vacant
Faces, we just jogged on, eternity
Gave itself airs in revolving lights
And then we came to the Thames and all
The bridges were down, the further shore
Was lost in fog, so we asked the conductor
What we should do. He said: Take the ferry
Faute de mieux. We flicked the flashlight
And there was the ferryman just as Virgil
And Dante had seen him. He looked at us coldly
And his eyes were dead and his hands on the oar
Were black with obols and varicose veins
Marbled his calves and he said to us coldly:
If you want to die you will have to pay for it.

BALLAD OF THE LONDONER

Evening falls on the smoky walls,
    And the railings drip with rain,
And I will cross the old river
    To see my girl again.

The great and solemn-gliding tram,
    Love's still-mysterious car,
Has many a light of gold and white,
    And a single dark red star.

I know a garden in a street
    Which no one ever knew;
I know a rose beyond the Thames
    Where flowers are pale and few.

'DELECTABLE CREATURES'

You won't remember, but it was
October and the street trees
still coloured like rude bouquets.
I had some rare walks by the river,
the weak sun loose on the water
and the light so washed out and lovely
it would make you cry if you weren't
completely alert. Every step I took
they were uncovering something: people
sleeping under cardboard, a lost riverboat
marooned on a freak low tide, the metal flotsam
which made metal detectors buzz, theatres
with resonant names: the Rose, the Globe.

And I was carrying a torch for someone
to the point of hallucination:
we rolled in flames through seven fields, the burning
so thorough I longed to be shocked by water,
a faceful of anything, even the smelly Thames.

And I remember the press full of doctors,
of inventions; a herringbone fragment
of DNA to fool a virus, a wisp
of vitamin to lock on to inner decay

and knock it dead for good. We were
saving vouchers, too, for air miles.

There was, O yes, the morning I woke up
to see an open book, drying on the drainer.
Dimly reconstructing the night before
I remembered dropping off, head on the desk,
getting up moments later, to select the book
with extra-exquisite care from any old shelf.
I slowly chose a page, spread it with jam
and butter, and tried to stuff it down my mouth.
It was, of course, Freud's *Jokes and the Unconscious*.
I must have tried to wash it like a tea plate,
stacked it, then put myself into my bed.

I think the explanation could be this:
that in the light, the river was sometimes pink,
and St. Paul's was pink, and even Lloyd's
in the distance was pink, as I crossed Waterloo Bridge
with a purchase under my arm, some piece
of frou frou or a novel to bring me back
from the seven fields, back to the river-mist
which must once have been river water, back
to breathing mist so deeply I could feel
each droplet hit my diaphragm like a shot.

LONDON SEAGULLS

The pigeons of the Abbey, the pigeons of Saint Paul's,
That woo in windy niches of grey and grimy walls,
The pearl-grey dawns of London, his sky that gleams
    and glooms,
His stately smoky sunsets are in their changing
    plumes.

The saucy London sparrows, their Cockney chatter
    tells
Their parents nested surely in earshot of Bow
    Bells . . .
But Oh! the London seagulls a-cruising up and down,
They're most like old-time seamen come back to
    London town.

Old salty swearing seadogs and tarry buccaneers,
With bacca quids and pigtails and ear-rings in their
    ears,
That spent their money handsome and took their ease
    ashore
In rowdy Ratcliff aleshops with sand upon the
    floor . . .

And bawled their old sea-ballads, and told their
    thumping lies,
In fearsome deep sea lingo to open landsmen's eyes,
And drained their brimming pewters, and spat into
    the tide,
In old shipboarded taverns by Wapping waterside . . .

And saw there at their moorings the Geordie colliers
    rock,
The latest pirate dangling at Execution Dock,
The anchored ships unloading their silks and laces
    fine,
And spices from the Indies, and rum, and Spanish
    wine . . .

And watched the busy wherries all plying with their
    fares,
From Globe, Jamaica, Wapping and Cherry Garden
    Stairs,
And the lighters and the barges a-passing to and fro
As they did on London River two hundred years ago.

SHADWELL STAIR

I am the ghost of Shadwell Stair,
 Along the wharves by the water-house
 And through the cavernous slaughter-house,
I am the shadow that walks there.

Yet I have flesh both firm and cool,
 And eyes tumultuous as the gems
 Of moons and lamps in the lapping Thames
When dusk sails wavering down the Pool.

Shuddering, a purple street-arc burns
 Where I watch always; from the banks
 Dolorously the shipping clanks,
And after me a strange tide turns.

I walk till the stars of London wane,
 And dawn creeps up the Shadwell Stair.
 But when the crowing sirens blare,
I with another ghost am lain.

WILFRED OWEN (1893–1918)   37

IN THE ISLE OF DOGS

While the water-wagon's ringing showers
Sweetened the dust with a woodland smell,
'Past noon, past noon, two sultry hours,'
Drowsily fell
From the schoolhouse clock
In the Isle of Dogs by Millwall Dock.

Mirrored in shadowy windows draped
With ragged net or half-drawn blind
Bowsprits, masts, exactly shaped
To woo or fight the wind,
Like monitors of guilt
By strength and beauty sent,
Disgraced the shameful houses built
To furnish rent.

From the pavements and the roofs
In shimmering volumes wound
The wrinkled heat;
Distant hammers, wheels and hoofs,
A turbulent pulse of sound,
Southward obscurely beat,
The only utterance of the afternoon,
Till on a sudden in the silent street

An organ-man drew up and ground
The Old Hundredth tune.

Forthwith the pillar of cloud that hides the past
Burst into flame,
Whose alchemy transmuted house and mast,
Street, dockyard, pier and pile:
By magic sound the Isle of Dogs became
A northern isle –
A green isle like a beryl set
In a wine-coloured sea,
Shadowed by mountains where a river met
The ocean's arm extended royally.

There also in the evening on the shore
An old man ground the Old Hundredth tune,
An old enchanter steeped in human lore,
Sad-eyed, with whitening beard, and visage lank:
Not since and not before,
Under the sunset or the mellowing moon,
Has any hand of man's conveyed
Such meaning in the turning of a crank.

Sometimes he played
As if his box had been
An organ in an abbey richly lit;
For when the dark invaded day's demesne,

And the sun set in crimson and in gold;
When idlers swarmed upon the esplanade,
And a late steamer wheeling towards the quay
Struck founts of silver from the darkling sea,
The solemn tune arose and shook and rolled
Above the throng,
Above the hum and tramp and bravely knit
All hearts in common memories of song.

Sometimes he played at speed;
Then the Old Hundredth like a devil's mass
Instinct with evil thought and evil deed,
Rang out in anguish and remorse. Alas!
That men must know both Heaven and Hell!
Sometimes the melody
Sang with the murmuring surge;
And with the winds would tell
Of peaceful graves and of the passing bell.
Sometimes it pealed across the bay
A high triumphal dirge,
A dirge
For the departing undefeated day.

A noble tune, a high becoming mate
Of the capped mountains and the deep broad firth;
A simple tune and great,
The fittest utterance of the voice of earth.

RISING DAMP
(*for C. A. K. and R. K. M.*)

A river can sometimes be diverted, but it is a very hard
thing to lose it altogether.
    – J. G. Head: *paper read to the Auctioneers' Institute in
       1907*

At our feet they lie low,
The little fervent underground
Rivers of London

Effra, Graveney, Falcon, Quaggy,
Wandle, Warbrook, Tyburn, Fleet

Whose names are disfigured,
Frayed, effaced.

These are the Magogs that chewed the clay
To the basin that London nestles in.
These are the currents that chiselled the city,
That washed the clothes and turned the mills,
Where children drank and salmon swam
And wells were holy.

They have gone under.
Boxed, like the magician's assistant.

Buried alive in earth.
Forgotten, like the dead.

They return spectrally after heavy rain,
Confounding suburban gardens. They infiltrate
Chronic bronchitis statistics. A silken
Slur haunts dwellings by shrouded
Watercourses, and is taken
For the footing of the dead.

Being of our world, they will return
(Westbourne, caged at Sloane Square,
Will jack from his box),
Will deluge cellars, detonate manholes,
Plant effluent on our faces,
Sink the city.

Effra, Graveney, Falcon, Quaggy,
Wandle, Walbrook, Tyburn, Fleet

It is the other rivers that lie
Lower, that touch us only in dreams
That never surface. We feel their tug
As a dowser's rod bends to the source below

Phlegethon, Acheron, Lethe, Styx.

From ON THE FAMOUS VOYAGE

[. .]   Great Club-fist, though thy back and
      bones be sore
Still, with thy former labours, yet once more
Act a brave work, call it thy last adventry;
But hold my torch while I describe the entry
To this dire passage. Say thou stop thy nose:
'Tis but light pains; indeed this dock's no rose.
    In the first jaws appeared that ugly monster
Ycleped Mud, which when their oars did once stir,
Belched forth an air as hot as at the muster
Of all your night-tubs, when the carts do cluster,
Who shall discharge first his merd-urinous load:
Thorough her womb they make their famous road
Between two walls, where on one side, to scare men
Were seen your ugly centaurs ye call car-men,
Gorgonian scolds and harpies; on the other
Hung stench, diseases, and old filth, their mother,
With famine, wants and sorrows many a dozen,
The least of which was to the plague a cousin.
But they unfrighted pass, though many a privy
Spake to 'em louder than the ox in Livy,
And many a sink poured out her rage anenst 'em;
But still their valour and their virtue fenced 'em,
And on they went [. .]

By this time they had reached the Stygian pool
Of worship, they their nodding chins do hit
Against their breasts. Here several ghosts did flit
About the shore, of farts but late departed,
White, black, blue, green, and in more forms
        out-started
Than all those atomi ridiculous
Whereof old Democrite and Hill Nicholas,
One said, the other swore, the world consists.
These be the cause of those thick frequent mists
Arising in that place, through which who goes
Must try the unused valour of a nose:
And that ours did. For yet no nare was tainted,
Nor thumb nor finger to the stop acquainted,
But open, and unarmed, encountered all.
Whether it languishing stuck upon the wall
Or were precipitated down the jakes,
And after swam abroad in ample flakes,
Or that it lay heaped like an usurer's mass,
All was to them the same: they were to pass,
And so they did, from Styx to Acheron,
The ever-boiling flood; whose banks upon
Your Fleet Lane furies and hot cooks do dwell,
That with still-scalding steams make the place hell.
[·]

WAILING IN WANDSWORTH

Lovers who would pet and fondle
All along the river Wandle,
Running down through Wandsworth Town
    Leafily, are gone.
Factory excreta tumble,
Gangs prowl, sniffing out a rumble,
    And the cops move on
Cottagers disposed to fumble
In their lowly dwelling, humble
    Public jakes or john.

Where the lovers used to ramble
Adult Aid chain owners amble,
Strolling down through Wandsworth Town,
    Counting up the cash.
By the bridge, his fourteenth tipple
Claims the drunk, who takes a triple
    Length-and-value slash,
And the alders wind would ripple,
Poplars, beech rain loves to stipple,
    Are not even ash.

Still and all, I shouldn't grumble,
I who sit alone and mumble,
Writing down in Wandsworth Town
    My troubled Double Dutch.
I would never cause to stumble
From its grave, but let it crumble,
    Ancient pain, as such.
By the waters of the Wandle
Where the lovers used to fondle,
Where I craft this rhubarb rondel,
    Life is better: much.

From PROTHALAMION

Calm was the day, and through the trembling air
Sweet breathing Zephyrus did softly play,
A gentle spirit, that lightly did delay
Hot Titan's beams, which then did glister fair;
When I, whose sullen care
Through discontent of my long fruitless stay
In prince's court, and expectation vain
Of idle hopes, which still do fly away
Like empty shadows, did afflict my brain,
Walked forth to ease my pain
Along the shore of silver streaming Thames,
Whose rutty bank, the which his river hems,
Was painted all with variable flowers,
And all the meads adorned with dainty gems,
Fit to deck maidens' bowers,
And crown their paramours,
Against the bridal day, which is not long:
  Sweet Thames run softly, till I end my song.

There in a meadow by the river's side,
A flock of nymphs I chancèd to espy,
All lovely daughters of the flood thereby,
With goodly greenish locks all loose untied,
As each had been a bride;
And each one had a little wicker basket,

Made of fine twigs entrailèd curiously,
In which they gathered flowers to fill their flasket,
And with fine fingers cropped full featously
The tender stalks on high.
Of every sort, which in that meadow grew,
They gathered some; the violet pallid blue,
The little daisy, that at evening closes,
The virgin lily, and the primrose true,
With store of vermeil roses,
To deck their bridegrooms' posies,
Against the bridal day which was not long:
    Sweet Thames run softly, till I end my song.

With that I saw two swans of goodly hue
Come softly swimming down along the Lee;
Two fairer birds I yet did never see.
The snow, which doth the top of Pindus strew,
Did never whiter shew,
Nor Jove himself, when he a swan would be
For love of Leda, whiter did appear:
Yet Leda was they say as white as he,
Yet not so white as these, nor nothing near.
So purely white they were,
That even the gentle stream, the which them bare,
Seemed foul to them, and bade his billows spare
To wet their silken feathers, lest they might
Soil their fair plumes with water not so fair,

And mar their beauties bright,
That shone as heaven's light,
Against their bridal day, which was not long:
    Sweet Thames, run softly, till I end my song.

Eftsoons the nymphs, which now had flowers their fill,
Ran all in haste to see that silver brood,
As they came floating on the crystal flood.
Whom when they saw, they stood amazéd still,
Their wondering eyes to fill.
Them seemed they never saw a sight so fair,
Of fowls so lovely, that they sure did deem
Them heavenly born, or to be that same pair
Which through the sky draw Venus' silver team;
For sure they did not seem
To be begot of any earthly seed,
But rather angels or of angels' breed:
Yet were they bred of Somers-heat they say,
In sweetest season, when each flower and weed
The earth did fresh array,
So fresh they seemed as day,
Even as their bridal day, which was not long:
    Sweet Thames, run softly, till I end my song.

Then forth they all out of their baskets drew
Great store of flowers, the honour of the field,
That to the sense did fragrant odours yield,

All which upon those goodly birds they threw,
And all the waves did strew,
That like old Peneus' waters they did seem,
When down along by pleasant Tempe's shore,
Scattered with flowers, through Thessaly they stream,
That they appear through lilies' plenteous store,
Like a bride's chamber floor. [. .]

From THE WASTE LAND

The river's tent is broken; the last fingers of leaf
Clutch and sink into the wet bank. The wind
Crosses the brown land, unheard. The nymphs are
    departed.
Sweet Thames, run softly, till I end my song.
The river bears no empty bottles, sandwich papers,
Silk handkerchiefs, cardboard boxes, cigarette ends
Or other testimony of summer nights. The nymphs
    are departed,
And their friends, the loitering heirs of City directors;
Departed, have left no addresses.
By the waters of Leman I sat down and wept . . .
Sweet Thames, run softly, till I end my song,
Sweet Thames, run softly, for I speak not loud or long.
But at my back in a cold blast I hear
The rattle of the bones, and chuckle spread from ear
    to ear.

A rat crept softly through the vegetation
Dragging its slimy belly on the bank
While I was fishing in the dull canal
On a winter evening round behind the gashouse
Musing upon the king my brother's wreck
And on the king my father's death before him.
White bodies naked on the low damp ground

And bones cast in a little low dry garret,
Rattled by the rat's foot only, year to year.
But at my back from time to time I hear
The sound of horns and motors, which shall bring
Sweeney to Mrs. Porter in the spring. [. .]

THE CITY AND WESTMINSTER

LONDON

London, thou art of townes A per se.
  Soveraign of cities, seemliest in sight,
Of high renoun, riches and royaltie;
  Of lordis, barons, and many a goodly knyght;
  Of most delectable lusty ladies bright;
Of famous prelatis, in habitis clericall;
  Of merchauntis full of substaunce and of myght:
London, thou art the flour of Cities all.

Gladdith anon, thou lusty Troynovaunt,
  Citie that some tyme cleped was New Troy;
In all the erth, imperiall as thou stant,
  Pryncesse of townes, of pleasure and of joy,
  A richer restith under no Christen roy;
For manly power, with craftis naturall,
  Fourmeth none fairer sith the flode of Noy:
London, thou art the flour of Cities all.

Gemme of all joy, jasper of jocunditie,
  Most myghty carbuncle of vertue and valour;
Strong Troy in vigour and in strenuytie;
  Of royall cities rose and geraflour;
  Empress of townes, exalt in honour;

In beawtie beryng the crone imperiall;
   Swete paradise precelling in pleasure;
London, thou art the flour of Cities all.

Above all ryvers thy Ryver hath renowne,
   Whose beryall stremys, pleasaunt and preclare,
Under thy lusty wallys renneth down,
   Where many a swan doth swymme with wyngis
      fair;
   Where many a barge doth saile and row with are;
Where many a ship doth rest with top-royall.
   O, towne of townes! patrone and not compare,
London, thou art the flour of Cities all.

Upon thy lusty Brigge of pylers white
   Been merchauntis full royall to behold;
Upon thy stretis goeth many a semely knyght
   In velvet gownes and in cheynes of gold.
   By Julyus Cesar thy Tour founded of old
May be the hous of Mars victoryall,
   Whose artillary with tonge may not be told:
London, thou art the flour of Cities all.

Strong be thy wallis that about thee standis;
   Wise be the people that within thee dwellis;
Fresh is thy ryver with his lusty strandis;
   Blith be thy chirches, wele sownyng be thy bellis;

Rich be thy merchauntis in substaunce that excellis;
Fair be their wives, right lovesom, white and small;
 Clere be thy virgyns, lusty under kellis:
London, thou art the flour of Cities all.

Thy famous Maire, by pryncely governaunce,
 With sword of justice thee ruleth prudently.
No Lord of Parys, Venyce, or Floraunce
 In dignitye or honour goeth to hym nigh.
 He is exampler, loode-ster, and guye;
Principall patrone and rose orygynalle,
 Above all Maires as maister most worthy:
London, thou art the flour of Cities all.

WILLIAM DUNBAR (1459–1520)

ORANGES AND LEMONS

Gay go up, and gay go down,
To ring the bells of London town.

Bull's eyes and targets,
Say the bells of St. Marg'ret's.

Brickbats and tiles,
Say the bells of St. Giles'.

Oranges and lemons,
Say the bells of St. Clement's.

Pancakes and fritters,
Say the bells of St. Peter's.

Two sticks and an apple,
Say the bells at Whitechapel.

Old Father Baldpate,
Say the slow bells at Aldgate.

Maids in white aprons,
Say the bells at St. Catherine's.

Pokers and tongs,
Say the bells at St. John's.

Kettles and pans,
Say the bells at St. Anne's.

You owe me five farthings,
Say the bells of St. Martin's.

When will you pay me,
Say the bells at Old Bailey.

When I grow rich,
Say the bells at Shoreditch.

Pray, when will that be?
Say the bells at Stepney.

I'm sure I don't know,
Says the great bell at Bow.

Here comes a candle to light you to bed,
And here comes a chopper to chop off your head.

From THE WASTE LAND

    Unreal City,
Under the brown fog of a winter dawn,
A crowd flowed over London Bridge, so many,
I had not thought death had undone so many.
Sighs, short and infrequent, were exhaled,
And each man fixed his eyes before his feet.
Flowed up the hill and down King William Street,
To where Saint Mary Woolnoth kept the hours
With a dead sound on the final stroke of nine.

From SUMMONED BY BELLS

All silvery on frosty Sunday nights
Were City steeples white against the stars.
And narrowly the chasms wound between
Italianate counting-houses, Roman banks,
To this church and to that. Huge office-doors,
Their granite thresholds worn by weekday feet
(Now far away in slippered ease at Penge),
Stood locked. St. Botolph this, St. Mary that
Alone shone out resplendent in the dark.
I used to stand by intersecting lanes
Among the silent offices, and wait,
Choosing which bell to follow: not a peal,
For that meant somewhere active; not St. Paul's,
For that was too well-known. I liked things dim –
Some lazy Rector living in Bexhill
Who most unwillingly on Sunday came
To take the statutory services.
A single bell would tinkle down a lane:
My echoing steps would track the source of sound –
A cassocked verger, bell-rope in his hands,
Called me to high box-pews, to cedar wood
(Like incense where no incense ever burned),
To ticking gallery-clock, and charity bench,
And free seats for the poor, and altar-piece –

Gilded Commandment boards – and sword-rests
　　made
For long-discarded aldermanic pomp.
A hidden organist sent reedy notes
To flute around the plasterwork. I stood,
And from the sea of pews a single head
With cherries nodding on a black straw hat
Rose in the neighbouring pew. The caretaker?
Or the sole resident parishioner?
And so once more, as for three hundred years,
This carven wood, these grey memorial'd walls
Heard once again the Book of Common Prayer,
While somewhere at the back the verger, now
Turned Parish Clerk, would rumble out 'Amen.'

THE BELLS

Boozy Boudicca has lost her brassiere
  on bonus day in Cornhill. Flush, cashed-up,
boozy and bloke-ish, Boudicca and I
  are serviced by the perma-tanned Slovenian
in T. M. Lewin. One straight line
  from Bank to boudoir via Spaceship Gherkin
whose footprint is studded by leapable bollards
  and historical CSR bollocks; bulging green,
dwarfing Botolph's classical resolve, where looped,
  Bangla-style, by a grey Mercedes, both of us
in exactly the right place. And so: the bells
  sound out, quite pished, across the City
as boobless Boudicca calculates a hangover
  to be a riskable asset in a recession.

TOM CHIVERS (1983–)

From THE ANATHEMATA:
'THE LADY OF THE POOL'

Did ever he walk the twenty-six wards of the city,
within and extra, did he cast his nautic eye on her
                              clere and lusty under kell
in the troia'd lanes of the city?
And was it but a month and less from the septimal
month, and did he hear, seemly intuned in *East-Seaxna*-
nasal

        (whose nestle-cock *polis* but theirs knows the
sweet gag and in what *urbs* would he hear it if not in
Belin's *oppidum,* the greatest *burh* in the nordlands?)
    Who'll try my sweet prime lavendula
    I cry my introit in a Dirige-*time*
    Come buy for summer's weeds, threnodic stalks
    For in Jane's ditch Jack will soon white his earliest rime
        Come, come buy
                good for a ditty-box, my fish-eye
        good to sweeten y'r poop-bower, cap'n.
        Come buy
                or else y'r duck'ill cry.
        Come buy my sweet lavender
                that bodes the fall-gale westerlies
        and ice on slow old Baldpate
        when the Nore gulls fly this way that tell to Lear's
        river a long winter's tale.

CITY STREET CRIES
(From *London Lick-Penny*)

In to London I gan me hy;
Of all the lond it bearethe the prise.
'Hot pescods!' one gan cry,
'Strabery rype, and chery in the ryse!'
One bad me come nere and by some spice;
Pepar and saffron they gan me bede,
Clove, grayns, and flowre of rise.
For lacke of money I might not spede.

Then into Chepe I gan me drawne,
Where I sawe stond moche people.
One bad me come nere, and by fine cloth of lawne,
Paris thred, coton, and umple.
I seyde there-upon I could no skyle,
I am not wont there-to in dede.
One bad me by an hewre, my hed to hele:
For lake of money I might not spede.

Then went I forth by London Stone
Thrwghe-out all Canywike strete.
Drapers to me they called anon;
Grete chepe of clothe, they gan me hete;
Then come there one, and cried 'Hot shepes fete!'
'Risshes faire and grene,' an othar began to grete;

Both melwell and makarell I gan mete,
But for lacke of money I myght not spede.

Then I hied me into Estchepe.
One cried, 'Ribes of befe, and many a pie!'
Pewtar potts they clatteryd on a heape.
Ther was harpe, pipe and sawtry.
'Ye by Cokke!' 'Nay by Cokke!' some began to cry;
Some sange of Jenken and Julian, to get themselvs
    mede.
Full fayne I wold hadd of that mynstralsie,
But for lacke of money I cowld not spede.

Into Cornhill anon I yode
Where is moche stolne gere amonge.
I saw wher henge myne owne hode
That I had lost in Westminstar amonge the throng.
Then I beheld it with lokes full longe;
I kenned it as well as I dyd my Crede.
To be myne owne hode agayne, me thought it wrong,
But for lacke of money I might not spede.

Then came the taverner, and toke my by the sleve,
And seyd, 'Ser, a pint of wyn would yow assay?'
'Syr,' quod I, 'it may not greve;
For a peny may do no more then it may.'
I dranke a pint, and therefore gan pay;

Sore a-hungred away I yede;
For well London Lykke-peny for ones and eye,
For lake of money I may not spede.

Then I hyed me to Byllingesgate,
And cried 'Wagge, wagge yow hens!'
I praye a barge man, for Gods sake,
That they would spare me myn expens.
He sayde, 'Ryse up, man, and get the hens.
What wenist thow I will do on the my almes-dede?
Here skapethe no man, by-nethe ij. pens!'
For lacke of money I myght not spede.

From MASTER FRANCIS BEAUMONT'S
LETTER TO BEN JONSON

                What things have we seen
Done at the Mermaid! heard words that have been
So nimble and so full of subtle flame,
As if that everyone from whence they came
Had meant to put his whole wit in a jest,
And had resolved to live a fool the rest
Of his dull life; then when there has been thrown
Wit able enough to justify the town
For three days past; wit that might warrant be
For the whole city to talk foolishly
Till that were cancelled, and when we were gone,
We left an air behind, which was alone
Able to make the two next companies
Right witty, though they were downright cockneys.

LINES ON THE MERMAID TAVERN

Souls of Poets dead and gone,
What Elysium have ye known,
Happy field or mossy cavern,
Choicer than the Mermaid Tavern?
Have ye tippled drink more fine
Than mine host's Canary wine?
Or are fruits of Paradise
Sweeter than those dainty pies
Of venison? O generous food!
Drest as though bold Robin Hood
Would, with his maid Marian,
Sup and bowse from horn and can.

I have heard that on a day
Mine host's sign-board flew away,
Nobody knew whither, till
An astrologer's old quill
To a sheepskin gave the story,
Said he saw you in your glory,
Underneath a new old sign
Sipping beverage divine,
And pledging with contented smack
The Mermaid in the Zodiac.

Souls of Poets dead and gone,
What Elysium have ye known,
Happy field or mossy cavern,
Choicer than the Mermaid Tavern?

PLAGUE
From *The Triumph of Death*

London now smokes with vapours that arise
　　From his foul sweat, himself he so bestirs:
'Cast out your dead!' the carcase-carrier cries,
　　Which he by heaps in groundless graves inters.

Now like to bees in summer's heat from hives,
　　Out fly the citizens, some here, some there;
Some all alone, and others with their wives:
　　With wives and children some fly, all for fear.

Here stands a watch, with guard of partisans,
　　To stop their passages, or to or fro,
As if they were not men, nor Christians,
　　But fiends or monsters, murdering as they go.

Each village, free, now standing on her guard,
　　None must have harbour in them but their own;
And as for life and death all watch and ward,
　　And fly for life (as death) the man unknown.

Here cry the parents for their children's death,
　　There howl the children for the parents' loss,
And often die as they are drawing breath
　　To cry for their but now inflicted cross.

The last survivor of a family
    Which yesterday, perhaps, were all in health,
Now dies to bear his fellows company,
    And for a grave for all gives all their wealth.

The London lanes (thereby themselves to save)
    Did vomit out their undigested dead,
Who by cart-loads are carried to the grave;
    For all these lanes with folk were overfed.
[. .]
Now fall the people into public fast,
    And all assemble in the church to pray;
Early and late their souls there take repast,
    As if preparing for a later day.

The pastors now steep all their words in brine,
    With 'woe, woe, woe,' – and nought is heard but
        woe:
'Woe and alas!' they say 'the powers divine
    Are bent mankind, for sin, to overthrow!'

'Repent, repent,' (like Jonas, now they cry)
    'Ye men of England! O repent, repent,
To see if ye may move pity's eye
    To look upon you ere you quite be spent.'

And oft while he breathes out these bitter words,
   He drawing breath draws in more bitter bane;
And now the air no air, but death affords,
   And lights of art (for help) were in the wane.

A LITANY IN TIME OF PLAGUE

Adieu, farewell, earth's bliss;
The world uncertain is;
Fond are life's lustful joys;
Death proves them all but toys;
None from his darts can fly;
I am sick, I must die.
   Lord, have mercy on us!

Rich men, trust not in wealth,
Gold cannot buy you health;
Physic himself must fade.
All things to end are made,
The plague full swift goes by;
I am sick, I must die.
   Lord, have mercy on us!

Beauty is but a flower
Which wrinkles will devour;
Brightness falls from the air;
Queens have died young and fair;
Dust hath closed Helen's eye.
I am sick, I must die.
   Lord, have mercy on us!

Strength stoops unto the grave,
Worms feed on Hector brave;
Swords may not fight with fate,
Earth still holds open her gate.
'Come, come!' the bells do cry.
I am sick, I must die.
    Lord, have mercy on us!

Wit with his wantonness
Tasteth death's bitterness;
Hell's executioner
Hath no ears for to hear
What vain art can reply.
I am sick, I must die.
    Lord, have mercy on us!

Haste, therefore, each degree,
To welcome destiny;
Heaven is our heritage,
Earth but a player's stage;
Mount we unto the sky.
I am sick, I must die.
    Lord, have mercy on us!

THE FIRE OF LONDON
From *Annus Mirabilis*

[. .]
In this deep quiet, from what source unknown,
  Those seeds of fire their fatal birth disclose:
And first few scattering sparks about are blown,
  Big with the flames that to our ruin rose.

Then, in some close-pent room it crept along,
  And, smouldering as it went, in silence fed:
Till the infant monster, with devouring strong,
  Walked boldly upright with exalted head.

Now, like some rich or mighty murderer,
  Too great for prison, which he breaks with gold,
Who fresher for new mischiefs does appear,
  And dares the world to tax him with the old;

So scapes the insulting fire his narrow gaol,
  And makes small outlets into open air:
There the fierce winds his tender force assail,
  And beat him downward to his first repair.

The winds, like crafty courtesans, withheld
　　His flames from burning but to blow them more:
And, every fresh attempt, he is repelled
　　With faint denials, weaker than before.

And now, no longer letted of his prey,
　　He leaps up at it with enraged desire,
O'erlooks the neighbours with a wide survey
　　And nods at every house his threatening fire.

The ghosts of traitors from the bridge descend
　　With bold fanatic spectres to rejoice;
About the fire into a dance they bend,
　　And sing their sabbath notes with feeble voice.

Our guardian angel saw them where he sate
　　Above the palace of our slumbering king:
He sighed, abandoning his charge to fate,
　　And, drooping, oft looked back upon the wing.

At length the crackling noise and dreadful blaze
　　Called up some waking lover to the sight;
And long it was ere he the rest could raise,
　　Whose heavy eyelids yet were full of night.

The next to danger, hot pursued by fate,
    Half-clothed, half-naked, hastily retire;
And frighted mothers strike their breasts, too late,
    For helpless infants left amidst the fire.

Their cries soon waken all the dwellers near;
    Now murmuring voices rise in every street;
The more remote run stumbling with their fear,
    And in the dark men jostle as they meet.

So weary bees in little cells repose;
    But if night-robbers lift the well-stored hive,
A humming through their waxen city grows,
    And out upon each other's wings they drive.

Now streets grow thronged and busy as by day;
    Some run for buckets to the hallowed choir;
Some cut the pipes, and some the engines play,
    And some more bold mount ladders to the fire.

In vain; for from the east a Belgian wind
    His hostile breath through the dry rafters sent;
The flames impelled soon left their foes behind,
    And forward with a wanton fury went.

A quay of fire ran all along the shore,
    And lightened all the river with a blaze;
The wakened tides began again to roar,
    And wondering fish in shining waters gaze.

Old Father Thames raised up his reverend head,
    But feared the fate of Simois would return;
Deep in his ooze he sought his sedgy bed,
    And shrank his waters back into his urn.

The fire, meantime, walks in a broader gross;
    To either hand his wings he opens wide;
He wades the streets, and straight he reaches cross
    And plays his longing flames on the other side.

At first they warm, then scorch, and then they take;
    Now with long necks from side to side they feed;
At length, grown strong, their mother-fire forsake,
    And a new colony of flames succeed.

To every nobler portion of the town
    The rolling billows roll their restless tide;
In parties now they straggle up and down,
    As armies, unopposed, for prey divide.

One mighty squadron, with a side-wind sped,
    Through narrow lanes his cumbered fire does haste,
By powerful charms of gold and silver led
    The Lombard bankers and the Change to waste.

Another backward to the Tower would go,
    And slowly eats his way against the wind;
But the main body of the marching foe
    Against the imperial palace is designed.

Now day appears, and with the day the king,
    Whose early care had robbed him of his rest:
Far off the cracks of falling houses ring,
    And shrieks of subjects pierce his tender breast.
[· ·]

ST. STEPHEN WALBROOK
From *Nairn's London*

God's crossword puzzle, Ximenes-by-the-Mansion-House. The clues have been so beautifully analysed by Nikolaus Pevsner in *An Outline of European Architecture* that there is no point in paraphrase. Wren here combined four church plans in one. St. Stephen's is a domed space, a nave and aisles, an even array of columns around a central hall, and a Greek cross, all at once. What it lacks is something which will tear your heart out, and for that you need to go a few yards farther east, to St. Mary Woolnoth. The coolness and balance at once created the intellectual marvel and prevented it from making the final leap. 'Spatial polyphony', as Dr. Pevsner said, but not worthy of Purcell, who never forgot his heart, but of J. S. Bach, who sometimes mislaid his. Yet it is not heartless but heart-free, in a landscape of detachment where neither pain nor pleasure has any meaning. It is, surely, one of the mansions – though it could never be mine.

IAN NAIRN (1930–83)   81

HOLY THURSDAY

'Twas on a Holy Thursday, their innocent faces clean,
The children walking two & two, in red & blue &
 green,
Grey-headed beadles walk'd before, with wands as
 white as snow,
Till into the high dome of Paul's they like Thames'
 waters flow.

O what a multitude they seem'd, these flowers of
 London town!
Seated in companies they sit with radiance all
 their own.
The hum of multitudes was there, but multitudes
 of lambs,
Thousands of little boys & girls raising their innocent
 hands.

Now like a mighty wind they raise to heaven the voice
 of song,
Or like harmonious thunderings the seats of heaven
 among.
Beneath them sit the aged men, wise guardians of
 the poor;
Then cherish pity, lest you drive an angel from
 your door.

A FEW WORDS FROM
REV. SYDNEY SMITH

He said that when he preached in St. Paul's in winter
his sentences froze in the air around the place
and suggested they came to rest as lumps of ice
in crevices and corners, on pediments,
waiting to melt with the warmer air of summer,
'making strange noises and unexpected assertions
in various parts of the church,' so that a woman
would hear, while crossing the nave, a long-drawn
    'furthermore'
from above the clerestory, a family in the Whispering
    Gallery
would experience the endless groan of an 'Oh'
while 'a rooted horror of war' might seep down
    the walls
of the crypt and be lost in the silence, as lost as
    his words
as he stabbed his stick across a crocus
struggling up through the frost-crust on a lawn,
'See, the resurrection of the world,'
or a visiting curate would start as he heard the phrase
'We may meet no more' thaw out in the choir.

PETER BOSTOCK (1929–2016)

IN ST. PAUL'S A WHILE AGO

Summer and winter close commune
On this July afternoon
As I enter chilly Paul's,
With its chasmal classic walls.
– Drifts of gray illumination
From the lofty fenestration
Slant them down in bristling spines that spread
Fan-like upon the vast dust-moted shade.

Moveless here, no whit allied
To the daemonian din outside,
Statues stand, cadaverous, wan,
Round the loiterers looking on
Under the yawning dome and nave,
Pondering whatnot, giddy or grave.
Here a verger moves a chair,
Or a red rope fixes there: –
A brimming Hebe, rapt in her adorning,
Brushes an Artemisia craped in mourning;
Beatrice Benedick piques, coquetting;
All unknowing, all forgetting
That strange Jew, Damascus-bound,
Whose name thereafter travelling round
To this precinct of the world,
Spread here like a flag unfurled:

Anon inspiring architectural sages
To frame this pile, writ his throughout the ages:
    Whence also the encircling mart
    Assumed his name, of him no part,
    And to his vision-seeking mind
    Charmless, blank in every kind;
And whose displays, even had they called his eye,
No gold or silver had been his to buy;
    Whose haunters, had they seen him stand
    On his own steps here, lift his hand
    In stress of eager, stammering speech,
    And his meaning chanced to reach,
    Would have proclaimed him as they passed
    An epilept enthusiast.

THOMAS HARDY (1840–1928)

HOMAGE TO WREN
A memory of 1941

At sea in the dome of St. Paul's
Riding the firefull night,
Fountains of sparks like a funfair,
We patrolled between the inner and outer walls,
Saw that all hatches were screwed down tight
And felt that Sir Christopher Wren had made
      everything shipshape.

Then went on deck with the spray
Of bombs in our ears and watched
The fire clouds caught in our rigging, the gaudy
      signals:
London Expects – but the rest of the string was
      vague,
Ambiguous rather and London was rolling away
Three hundred years to the aftermath of the plague,

And the flames were whippeting, dolphining, over the
      streets,
The red whale spouting out of submerged Londinium
And Davy Jones's locker burst wide open
To throw to the surface ledgers and lavatory seats
And all the bric-a-brac of warehouses and churches
With bones and ghosts and half forgotten quotations.

Then the storm subsided and it was dawn, it was cold,
I climbed to the crow's nest for one last look at the
    roaring foam,
League upon league of scarlet and gold,
But it was cold so I stretched out my hands from the
    drunken mast
And warmed my hands at London and went home.

LOUIS MacNEICE (1907–63)

FLEET STREET

Beneath this narrow jostling street,
Unruffled by the noise of feet,
Like a slow organ-note I hear
The pulses of the great world beat.

Unseen beneath the city's show
Through this aorta ever flow
The currents of the universe –
A thousand pulses throbbing low!

Unheard beneath the pavement's din
Unknown magicians sit within
Dim caves, and weave life into words
On patient looms that spin and spin.

There, uninspired, yet with the dower
Of mightier mechanic power,
Some bent, obscure Euripides
Builds the loud drama of the hour!

There, from the gaping presses hurled,
A thousand voices, passion-whirled,
With throats of steel vociferate
The incessant story of the world!

So through this artery from age
To age the tides of passion rage,
The swift historians of each day
Flinging a world upon a page!

And then I pause and gaze my fill
Where cataracts of traffic spill
Their foam into the Circus. Lo!
Look up, the crown on Ludgate Hill!

Remote from all the city's moods,
In high, untroubled solitudes,
Like an old Buddha swathed in dream,
St. Paul's above the city broods!

ARTHUR HENRY ADAMS (1872–1936)

LONDON

I wander thro' each charter'd street,
Near where the charter'd Thames does flow,
And mark in every face I meet
Marks of weakness, marks of woe.

In every cry of every Man,
In every Infant's cry of fear,
In every voice, in every ban,
The mind-forg'd manacles I hear.

How the Chimney-sweeper's cry
Every black'ning Church appalls;
And the hapless Soldier's sigh
Runs in blood down Palace walls.

But most thro' midnight streets I hear
How the youthful Harlot's curse
Blasts the new born Infant's tear,
And blights with plagues the Marriage hearse.

HELL
From *Peter Bell the Third*

Hell is a city much like London –
　　A populous and smoky city;
There are all sorts of people undone,
And there is little or no fun done;
　　Small justice shown, and still less pity.

There is a Castles and a Canning,
　　A Cobbett, and a Castlereagh;
All sorts of caitiff corpses planning
All sorts of cozening for trepanning
　　Corpses less corrupt than they.

There is a ***, who has lost
　　His wits, or sold them, none knows which;
He walks about a double ghost,
And though as thin as Fraud almost –
　　Ever grows more grim and rich.

There is a Chancery Court; a King;
　　A manufacturing mob; a set
Of thieves who by themselves are sent
Similar thieves to represent;
　　An army; and a public debt.

Which last is a scheme of paper money,
    And means – being interpreted –
'Bees, keep your wax – give us the honey,
And we will plant, while skies are sunny,
    Flowers, which in winter serve instead.'

There is a great talk of revolution –
    And a great chance of despotism –
German soldiers – camps – confusion –
Tumults – lotteries – rage – delusion –
    Gin – suicide – and methodism;

Taxes too, on wine and bread,
    And meat, and beer, and tea, and cheese,
From which those patriots pure are fed,
Who gorge before they reel to bed
    The tenfold essence of all these.

There are mincing women, mewing
    (Like cats, who *amant misere,*)
Of their own virtue, and pursuing
Their gentler sisters to that ruin,
    Without which – what were chastity?

Lawyers – judges – old hobnobbers
    Are there – bailiffs – chancellors –
Bishops – great and little robbers –
Rhymesters – pamphleteers – stock-jobbers –
    Men of glory in the wars, –

Things whose trade is, over ladies
    To lean, and flirt, and stare, and simper,
Till all that is divine in woman
Grows cruel, courteous, smooth, inhuman,
    Crucified 'twixt a smile and whimper.

Thrusting, toiling, wailing, moiling,
    Frowning, preaching – such a riot!
Each with never-ceasing labour,
Whilst he thinks he cheats his neighbour,
    Cheating his own heart of quiet.

And all these meet at levees; –
    Dinners convivial and political; –
Suppers of epic poets; – teas,
Where small talk dies in agonies; –
    Breakfasts professional and critical;

Lunches and snacks so aldermanic
   That one would furnish forth ten dinners,
Where reigns a Cretan-tonguèd panic,
Lest news Russ, Dutch, or Alemannic
   Should make some losers, and some winners; –

At conversazioni – balls –
   Conventicles – and drawing-rooms –
Courts of law – committees – calls
Of a morning – clubs – book-stalls –
   Churches – masquerades – and tombs.

And this is Hell – and in this smother
   All are damnable and damned;
Each one damning, damns the other;
They are damned by one another,
   By none other are they damned.

THE PRINCES IN THE TOWER
From The Tragedy of Richard the Third

Enter Tyrrel

TYRREL: The tyrannous and bloody act is done,
  The most arch deed of piteous massacre
  That ever yet this land was guilty of.
  Dighton and Forrest, who I did suborn
  To do this piece of ruthful butchery,
  Albeit they were fleshed villains, bloody dogs,
  Melted with tenderness and mild compassion,
  Wept like to children in their death's sad story.
  'O thus,' quoth Dighton, 'lay the gentle babes.'
  'Thus, thus,' quoth Forrest, 'girdling one
        another
  Within their alabaster innocent arms.
  Their lips were four red roses on a stalk
  And in their summer beauty kissed each other.
  A book of prayers on their pillow lay,
  Which once,' quoth Forrest, 'almost changed my
        mind;
  But O, the devil' – there the villain stopped;
  When Dighton thus told on: 'We smotherèd
  The most replenishèd sweet work of Nature
  That from the prime creation e'er she framed.'
  Hence both are gone with conscience and remorse

They could not speak; and so I left them both,
To bear this tidings to the bloody king.

Enter Richard

And here he comes. All health, my sovereign Lord!

KING RICHARD: Kind Tyrrel, am I happy in thy news?

TYRREL: If to have done the thing you gave in charge
Beget your happiness, be happy then,
For it is done.

KING RICHARD: But didst thou see them dead?

TYRREL: I did, my lord.

KING RICHARD: And buried, gentle Tyrrel?

TYRREL: The chaplain of the Tower hath buried
them;
But where (to say the truth) I do not know.

KING RICHARD: Come to me, Tyrrel, soon at after-
supper,
When thou shalt tell the process of their death.
Meantime, but think how I may do thee good

And be inheritor of thy desire.
Farewell till then.

TYRREL: I humbly take my leave.   ⌈Exit⌉

LITTLE EASE

Lubricious brass winks at iron.
Julie stands by the daughter,
A grin ripping her mouth
And her eyes red-balled
In the flash.

Skevington devised his machine
When Lieutenant of the Tower.
It compressed and doubled
The victim's body,
Forcing the head to the feet.

Nose and ears jerked blood,
Sometimes fingers and toes.
The machine was named
Skevington's Daughter
Or Little Ease.

Julie posed there some seconds:
Seconds passing as seconds
Then her grin and the flash
Both leaping
The huge dumb flags of the floor.

98   OLIVER REYNOLDS (1957–)

'WHO LIST HIS WEALTH
AND EASE RETAIN'

Who list his wealth and ease retain,
Himself let him unknown contain;
Press not too fast in at the gate
Where the return stands by disdain:
   For sure, *circa Regna tonat.*

The high mountains are blasted oft
When the low valley is mild and soft;
Fortune with health stands at debate,
The fall is grievous from aloft,
   And sure, *circa Regna tonat.*

These bloody days have broken my heart:
My lust, my youth, did then depart,
And blind desire of estate.
Who hastes to climb seeks to revert:
   Of truth, *circa Regna tonat.*

The bell-tower showed me such sight
That in my head sticks day and night:
There did I learn out of a grate,
For all favour, glory or might,
   That yet *circa Regna tonat.*

By proof, I say, there did I learn,
Wit helpeth not defence too yern,
Of innocency to plead or prate:
Bear low, therefore, give God the stern.
  For sure, *circa Regna tonat.*

From HOLBEIN

I

The other Cromwell, that strange muse of Wyatt
and master of last things: it makes a fine
edge – wisdom so near miswielding power.
I think of the headsman balancing that
extraordinary axe for a long instant
without breaking the skin; then the engine
cuts its ascending outline on the air,
wharrs its velocity, dreadful, perhaps
merciful. And that moment of spreading
the arms wide as a signal. In fact it's all
signals. Pray, sirs, remember Cromwell's trim
wit on the scaffold, that saved Wyatt's neck;
the one blubbing – talk of the *quiet mind*! –
the other a scoundrel, yet this redeems him.

PORTRAITS OF TUDOR STATESMEN

Surviving is keeping your eyes open,
Controlling the twitchy apparatus
Of iris, white, cornea, lash and lid.

So the literal painter set it down –
The sharp raptorial look; the strained eyeball;
And mail, ruff, bands, beard, anything, to hide
The violently vulnerable neck.

From FIRE: A SONG FOR
MISTRESS ASKEW

I set this fire in a hard frost: early evening, the garden's
winter leavings, the unretrievable, the piecemeal
    burdens.
Paraffin to start it – that dry *whoomph*! – and I saw
    her ghost
chained there: the woodcut from Foxe's 'Actes
and Monuments' that hung on the chapel wall
beside 'The Light of the World', a mild-mannered
    Christ,
his jaunty crown of thorns . . . The minister's stage-
    effects
were rage and unforgiveness, his colours red and red
    again
which were heart's-blood and hell-fire, the least of us
    already lost.
[. .]
That they gave her cripple water, that she ate
spoiled meat; that this was her penance, that she saw
those long nights through bedded on stone and straw;
that women in the garden by the White Tower
turned to one another, amazed: 'What is that animal?'
                      The river beat,
hour after hour as they racked her, back from the
    water gate.

[. .]

Then the pyre at Smithfield; those there to watch:
Norfolk, Bonner, Bowes, priests, judges, one and all
the Devil's dishwashers. Before they lit the stack,
Shaxton preached repentance. Broken, she listened.
The crowd stood round in a ring, ten deep, and felt
    the scorch.

[. .]

The frame of her in the fire, black to the bone.
    Her head
a smoking cinder, smiling, smiling, smiling.
Some stood close enough to catch the haul
and roar of flame in the summer wind as it fed,
close enough to hear the shrivel-hiss
of burning hair, to see her sag and slump, to witness
the pucker and slide of her skin, the blister-rash on
    her eyeballs.

From AN HORATIAN ODE UPON CROMWELL'S RETURN FROM IRELAND

[.]   And Hampton shows what part
     He had of wiser art;
Where, twining subtle fears with hope,
He wove a net of such a scope,
     That Charles himself might chase
     To Carisbrook's narrow case,
That thence the royal actor borne,
The tragic scaffold might adorn;
     While round the arméd bands
     Did clap their bloody hands.
He nothing common did, or mean,
Upon that memorable scene,
     But with his keener eye
     The axe's edge did try;
Nor called the gods with vulgar spite
To vindicate his helpless right;
     But bowed his comely head
     Down, as upon a bed.
This was that memorable hour,
Which first assured the forcéd power;
     So, when they did design
     The Capitol's first line,

A bleeding head, where they begun,
Did fright the architects to run;
 And yet in that the state
 Foresaw its happy fate.   [. .]

BY THE STATUE OF KING CHARLES
AT CHARING CROSS

Sombre and rich, the skies;
Great glooms, and starry plains.
Gently the night wind sighs;
Else a vast silence reigns.

The splendid silence clings
Around me: and around
The saddest of all kings
Crowned, and again discrowned.

Comely and calm, he rides
Hard by his own Whitehall:
Only the night wind glides:
No crowds, nor rebels, brawl.

Gone, too, his Court; and yet,
The stars his courtiers are:
Stars in their stations set;
And every wandering star.

Alone he rides, alone,
The fair and fatal king:
Dark night is all his own,
That strange and solemn thing.

Which are more full of fate:
The stars; or those sad eyes?
Which are more still and great:
Those brows; or the dark skies?

Although his whole heart yearn
In passionate tragedy:
Never was face so stern
With sweet austerity.

Vanquished in life, his death
By beauty made amends:
The passing of his breath
Won his defeated ends.

Brief life and hapless? Nay:
Through death, life grew sublime.
Speak after sentence? Yea:
And to the end of time.

Armoured he rides, his head
Bare to the stars of doom:
He triumphs now, the dead,
Beholding London's gloom.

Our wearier spirit faints,
Vexed in the world's employ:
His soul was of the saints;
And art to him was joy.

King, tried in fires of woe!
Men hunger for thy grace:
And through the night I go,
Loving thy mournful face.

Yet when the city sleeps;
When all the cries are still:
The stars and heavenly deeps
Work out a perfect will.

CLEVER TOM CLINCH, GOING
TO BE HANGED

As clever *Tom Clinch*, while the Rabble was bawling,
Rode stately through *Holbourn*, to die in his Calling;
He stopt at the *George* for a Bottle of Sack,
And promis'd to pay for it when he'd come back.
His Waistcoat and Stockings, and Breeches were white,
His Cap had a new Cherry Ribbon to ty't.
The Maids to the Doors and the Balconies ran,
And said, lack-a-day! he's a proper young Man.
But, as from the Windows the Ladies he spy'd,
Like a Beau in the Box, he bow'd low on each Side;
And when his last Speech the loud Hawkers did cry,
He swore from his Cart, it was all a damn'd Lye.
The Hangman for Pardon fell down on his Knee;
Tom gave him a Kick in the Guts for his Fee.
Then said, I must speak to the People a little,
But I'll see you all damn'd before I will *whittle*.
My honest Friend *Wild*, may he long hold his Place,
He lengthen'd my Life with a whole Year of Grace.
Take Courage, dear Comrades, and be not afraid,
Nor slip this Occasion to follow your Trade.
My Conscience is clear, and my Spirits are calm,
And thus I go off without Pray'r-Book or Psalm.
Then follow the Practice of clever *Tom Clinch*,
Who hung like a Hero, and never would flinch.

A BALLAD OF THE GOOD LORD NELSON

The Good Lord Nelson had a swollen gland,
Little of the scripture did he understand
Till a woman led him to the promised land
  Aboard the Victory, Victory O.

Adam and Evil and a bushel of figs
Meant nothing to Nelson who was keeping pigs,
Till a woman showed him the various rigs
  Aboard the Victory, Victory O.

His heart was softer than a new laid egg,
Too poor for loving and ashamed to beg,
Till Nelson was taken by the Dancing Leg
  Aboard the Victory, Victory O.

Now he up and did up his little tin trunk
And he took to the ocean on his English junk,
Turning like the hour-glass in his lonely bunk
  Aboard the Victory, Victory O.

The Frenchman saw him a-coming there
With the one-piece eye and the valentine hair,
With the safety-pin sleeve and occupied air
  Aboard the Victory, Victory O.

Now you all remember the message he sent
As an answer to Hamilton's discontent –
There were questions asked about it in Parliament
    Aboard the Victory, Victory O.

Now the blacker the berry, the thicker comes the juice.
Think of Good Lord Nelson and avoid self-abuse,
For the empty sleeve was no mere excuse
    Aboard the Victory, Victory O.

'England Expects' was the motto he gave
When he thought of little Emma out on Biscay's wave,
And remembered working on her like a galley-slave
    Aboard the Victory, Victory O.

The first Great Lord in our English land
To honour the Freudian command,
For a cast in the bush is worth two in the hand
    Aboard the Victory, Victory O.

Now the Frenchman shot him there as he stood
In the rage of battle in a silk-lined hood
And he heard the whistle of his own hot blood
    Aboard the Victory, Victory O.

Now stiff on a pillar with a phallic air
Nelson stylites in Trafalgar Square
Reminds the British what once they were
   Aboard the Victory, Victory O.

If they'd treat their women in the Nelson way
There'd be fewer frigid husbands every day
And many more heroes on the Bay of Biscay
   Aboard the Victory, Victory O.

VILLES
From *Les Illuminations*

The official acropolis outdoes the most colossal concep-
tions of modern barbarity. It is impossible to describe
the dull light produced by the unchanging grey sky,
the imperial brightness of the masonry, and the eter-
nal snow on the ground. They have reproduced, in
singularly outrageous taste, all the classical marvels
of architecture. I go to exhibitions of painting in places
twenty times vaster than Hampton Court. What
painting! A Norwegian Nebuchadnezzar designed the
staircases of the ministries; the minor officials I did see
are prouder than the Brahmins as it is, and the looks
of the guardians of colossi and of the building foremen
made me tremble. By their grouping of the buildings,
in closed squares, terraces, and courtyards, they have
squeezed out the bell-towers. The parks present prime-
val nature cultivated with marvellous art. [. .]

        TRANSLATED BY OLIVER BERNARD

BIG BEN

From *Mrs. Dalloway*

[.]

For having lived in Westminster – how many years now? over twenty – one feels even in the midst of the traffic, or waking at night, Clarissa was positive, a particular hush, or solemnity; an indescribable pause; a suspense (but that might be her heart, affected, they said, by influenza) before Big Ben strikes. There! Out it boomed. First a warning, musical; then the hour, irrevocable. The leaden circles dissolved in the air. Such fools we are, she thought, crossing Victoria Street. For Heaven only knows why one loves it so, how one sees it so, making it up, building it round one, tumbling it, creating it every moment afresh; but the veriest frumps, the most dejected of miseries sitting on doorsteps (drink their downfall) do the same; can't be dealt with, she felt positive, by Acts of Parliament for that very reason: they love life. In people's eyes, in the swing, tramp, and trudge; in the bellow and the uproar; the carriages, motor cars, omnibuses, vans, sandwich men shuffling and swinging; brass bands; barrel organs; in the triumph and the jingle and the strange high singing of some aeroplane overhead was what she loved; life; London; this moment of June.

[.]

WESTMINSTER ABBEY

Mortality, behold and fear!
What a change of flesh is here!
Think how many royal bones
Sleep within this heap of stones,
Hence removed from beds of ease,
Dainty fare, and what might please,
Fretted roofs, and costly shows,
To a roof that flats the nose:
Which proclaims all flesh is grass,
How the world's fair glories pass;
That there is no trust in health,
In youth, in age, in greatness, wealth:
For if such could have reprieved,
Those had been immortal lived.
Know from this the world a snare,
How that greatness is but care,
How all pleasures are but pain,
And how short they do remain:
For here they lie had realms and lands,
That now want strength to stir their hands;
Where from their pulpits sealed with dust
They preach, 'In greatness is no trust.'
Here's an acre sown indeed
With the richest royal'st seed
That the earth did e'er suck in

Since the first man died for sin;
Here the bones of birth have cried
'Though gods they were, as men they died.'
Here are sands, ignoble things,
Dropped from the ruin'd sides of Kings;
With whom the poor man's earth being shown,
The difference is not easily known.
Here's a world of pomp and state
Forgotten, dead, disconsolate.
Think then, this scythe, that mows down kings,
Exempts no meaner mortal things.
Then bid the wanton lady tread
Amid these mazes of the dead;
And these, truly understood,
More shall cool and quench the blood
Than her many sports a-day,
And her nightly wanton play:
Bid her paint till day of doom,
To this favour she must come.
Bid the merchant gather wealth,
The usurer exact by stealth,
The proud man beat it from his thought –
Yet to this shape all must be brought.

THE STATUES OF BUCKINGHAM PALACE

One day, old lion, we will stir ourselves,
shake off the bronze and be flesh.

The sash across my breast is blue I think, my hair
the dirty blonde of your pelt.

First we will look over our shoulders – I'll smile
shyly at the young men who've lounged a century

by the pool, then, without comment, you'll
roll your great shoulders and pad down onto the Mall.

I keep my hand warm in the rough tangle
of your mane. We walk past straight-backed generals

dusting the last of the black paint from their coats,
    while
the gentlemen of state adjust their breeches and steel

swords, clear their throats, and scramble down to the
    grass.
Along the Embankment we're joined by a few nervous

poets and the occasional nurse. The light is flat, Apollos
blink their olive eyes and begin to tune their lyres;

the muses and graces group with soft calls
to touch each other's pale new skins

with their fingertips. Mythical beasts lope beside us
and the Thames is full of mermaids in pearled scales.

We turn up towards Trafalgar Square, joined
by a Jesus or two, who have clambered

down from the fronts of churches. A little bemused,
    they rub
their palms and shiver. The military gentlemen give
    them overcoats,

clucking under their waxed moustaches. The Jesuses
    bob
their heads in thanks, feel in the pockets for tobacco.

Then everyone goes still to watch as you and I, old
    lion, climb the steps
to the Gallery and whisper steeply at the keyhole,
    waking the pictures.

DIVERSIONS

DIVERSIONS

From ON ST. JAMES'S PARK, AS LATELY IMPROVED BY HIS MAJESTY

Of the first paradise there's nothing found;
Plants sent by heaven are vanished, and the ground;
Yet the description lasts: who knows the fate
Of lines that shall this paradise relate?
   Instead of rivers rolling by the side
Of Eden's garden, here flows in the tide;
The sea, which always serves his empire, now
Pays tribute to our prince's pleasure too.
Of famous cities we the founders know;
But rivers, old as seas to which they go,
Are nature's bounty; 'tis of more renown
To make a river than to build a town.
   For future shade young trees upon the banks
Of the new stream appear in even ranks;
The voice of Orpheus, or Amphion's hand,
In better order could not make them stand;
May they increase as fast, and spread their boughs,
As the high fame of their great owner grows!
May he live long enough to see them all
Dark shadows cast, and as his palace tall!
Methinks I see the love that shall be made,
The lovers walking in that amorous shade,
The gallants dancing by the river's side;
They bathe in summer, and in winter slide.

Methinks I hear the music in the boats,
And the loud echo which returns the notes,
While overhead a flock of new-sprung fowl
Hangs in the air, and does the sun control,
Darkening the sky; they hover o'er, and shroud
The wanton sailors with a feathered cloud.
Beneath, a shoal of silver fishes glides,
And plays about the gilded barges' sides;
The ladies, angling in the crystal lake,
Feast on the waters with the prey they take,
At once victorious with their lines, and eyes,
They make the fishes, and the men, their prize.
A thousand Cupids on the billows ride,
And sea-nymphs enter with the swelling tide,
From Thetis sent as spies, to make report,
And tell the wonders of her sovereign's court.
[. .]

From A RAMBLE IN ST. JAMES'S PARK

Much wine had passed, with grave discourse
Of who fucks who, and who does worse,
Such as you usually do hear
From those that diet at the Bear;
When I, who still take care to see
Drunkenness relieved by lechery,
Went out into St. James's Park
To cool my head, and fire my heart.
But though St. James's has the honour on't,
'Tis consecrate to prick and cunt.
There, by a most incestuous birth,
Strange woods spring from the teeming earth:
For they relate how heretofore,
When ancient Pict began to whore,
Deluded of his assignation
(Jilting, it seems, was then in fashion),
Poor pensive lover, in this place
Would frig upon his mother's face;
Whence rows of mandrakes tall did rise,
Whose lewd tops fucked the very skies.
Each imitative branch did twine
In some loved fold of Aretine:
And nightly now beneath their shade
Are buggeries, rapes, and incest made.
Unto this all-sin-sheltering grove

Whores of the bulk and the alcove,
Great ladies, chamber-maids, and drudges,
The rag-picker and heiress trudges;
Car-men, divines, great lords, and tailors,
'Prentices, pimps, poets, and jailers,
Footmen, fine fops, do here arrive,
And here promiscuously they swive.

[. .]

THE GARDEN

En robe de parade.
– Samain.

Like a skein of loose silk blown against a wall
She walks by the railing of a path in Kensington
    Gardens,
And she is dying piece-meal
      of a sort of emotional anæmia.

And round about there is a rabble
Of the filthy, sturdy, unkillable infants of the
    very poor.
They shall inherit the earth.

In her is the end of breeding.
Her boredom is exquisite and excessive.
She would like some one to speak to her,
And is almost afraid that I
      will commit that indiscretion.

EZRA POUND (1885–1972)   127

QUEEN MARY'S ROSE GARDEN

In this day before the day nobody is about.
A sea of dreams washes the edge of my green island
In the center of the garden named after Queen Mary.
The great roses, many of them scentless,
Rule their beds like beheaded and resurrected and all
    silent royalty,
The only fare on my bare breakfast plate.

Such a waste of brightness I can't understand.
It is six in the morning and finer than any Sunday –
Yet there is no walker and looker but myself.
The sky of the city is white; the light from the
    country.
Some ducks step down off their green-reeded shelf
And into the silver element of the pond.

I see them start to cruise and dip for food
Under the bell-jar of a wonderland.
Hedged in and evidently inviolate
Though hundreds of Londoners know it like the palm
    of their hand.
The roses are named after queens and people of note
Or after gay days, or colors the grower found good.

And I have no intention of disparaging them
For being too well-bred and smelless and liking
    the city.
I enjoy petticoats and velvets and gossip of court,
And a titled lady may frequently be a beauty.
A Devon meadow might offer a simpler sort
Of personage – single-skirted, perfumed, a gem –
But I am content with this more pompous lot.

JAGUAR

The apes yawn and adore their fleas in the sun.
The parrots shriek as if they were on fire, or strut
Like cheap tarts to attract the stroller with the nut.
Fatigued with indolence, tiger and lion

Lie still as the sun. The boa-constrictor's coil
Is a fossil. Cage after cage seems empty, or
Stinks of sleepers from the breathing straw.
It might be painted on a nursery wall.

But who runs like the rest past these arrives
At a cage where the crowd stands, stares, mesmerized,
As a child at a dream, at a jaguar hurrying enraged
Through prison darkness after the drills of his eyes

On a short fierce fuse. Not in boredom –
The eye satisfied to be blind in fire,
By the bang of blood in the brain deaf the ear –
He spins from the bars, but there's no cage to him

More than to the visionary his cell:
His stride is wildernesses of freedom:
The world rolls under the long thrust of his heel.
Over the cage floor the horizons come.

SERENA I

without the grand old British Museum
Thales and the Aretino
on the bosom of the Regent's Park the phlox
crackles under the thunder
scarlet beauty in our world dead fish adrift
all things full of gods
pressed down and bleeding
a weaver-bird is tangerine the harpy is past caring
the condor likewise in his mangy boa
they stare out across monkey-hill the elephants
Ireland
the light creeps down their old home canyon
sucks me aloof to that old reliable
the burning btm of George the drill
ah across the way a adder
broaches her rat
white as snow
in her dazzling oven strom of peristalsis
limae labor

ah father father that art in heaven

I find me taking the Crystal Palace
for the Blessed Isles from Primrose Hill
alas I must be that kind of person

hence in Ken Wood who shall find me
my breath held in the midst of thickets
none but the most quarried lovers

I surprise me moved by the many a funnel hinged
for the obeisance to Tower Bridge
the viper's curtsy to and from the City
till in the dusk a lighter
blind with pride
tosses aside the scarf of the bascules
then in the grey hold of the ambulance
throbbing on the brink ebb of sighs
then I hug me below among the canaille
until a guttersnipe blast his cernèd eyes
demanding 'ave I done with the Mirror
I stump off in a fearful rage under Married Men's
        Quarters
Bloody Tower
and afar off at all speed screw me up Wren's giant
        bully
and curse the day caged panting on the platform
under the flaring urn
I was not born Defoe

but in Ken Wood
who shall find me

my brother the fly
the common housefly
sidling out of darkness into light
fastens on his place in the sun
whets his six legs
revels in his planes his poisers
it is the autumn of his life
he could not serve typhoid and mammon

HOMAGE TO THE BRITISH MUSEUM

There is a Supreme God in the ethnological section;
A hollow toad shape, faced with a blank shield.
He needs his belly to include the Pantheon,
Which is inserted through a hole behind.
At the navel, at the points formally stressed, at the
        organs of sense,
Lice glue themselves, dolls, local deities,
His smooth wood creeps with all the creeds of
        the world.

Attending there let us absorb the cultures of nations
And dissolve into our judgement all their codes.
Then, being clogged with a natural hesitation
(People are continually asking one the way out),
Let us stand here and admit that we have no road.
Being everything, let us admit that is to be something,
Or give ourselves to the benefit of the doubt;
Let us offer our pinch of dust all to this God,
And grant his reign over the entire building.

SONG OF THE TEMPLE MAIDEN

I shall step lightly over the curators, and neither disturb them in their nests nor cause them to fly.

Oh Museum, Museum! You whose very name means
    'Place of the Muse'.
Whose little friends scuttle round us as we work, yet
    chew not the exhibits.
Whose Department of Science and Conservation
    holds a Cyanide Room.
Whose Department of Coins and Medals tinkles
    when shaken.
Who cause veneration of the Roman and the Greek,
    if old.
Who uphold the Egyptian way of life. Which smiles
    through its bandages.
Whose Mesopotamian Ram is really a Billy Goat.
Whose Buddha Rooms whisper throughout the whole
    building.
Who would unwrap the secrets of everything dead.
Whose roof is high and clear and reaches the sky.
Who are built like a temple and preside gracefully
    over Bloomsbury.
Who hide somewhere the crystal ball of John Dee.
Whose bog-man lies dreaming forever, forever.

Who cradle the little children in your arms as they
    run through your galleries.
Who meet the gaze of the public with a stare that
    disinvents them.
Who are truly Neolithic at heart.
Who are in love with Time.
Who wish only to sleep under the sands of the desert
    (Gobi) for a thousand years.
Who sometimes perhaps, though not given to passion,
    cry at night-time
For the billions upon billions who have pressed
    momentarily upwards
Out of the yellow earth, pushing and myawling like
    kittens,
Eyes milky and blue, intent, only to sink back under
Leaving barely an impression, just a slight hollow, or
    a little mound,
Or a yellowed artefact bearing a list of cattle or corn
    in an unintelligible script.
Oh Museum, Museum! I pile white anemones onto
    your steps.
I pour out red wine onto your earth. I sacrifice
    nothing,
But release this small bird with a black mark on him
    and a mottled throat,
Whose voice is so pure that the poets praise him,

To fly up to your roof and lift up songs for you and
    please your ear
And perhaps even bring to your beautiful face an
    archaic smile.

IMPERIAL WAR MUSEUM, NOVEMBER

Podium and Ionic propylaeum,
Symbol of public-school civilization
Built post-Waterloo on the site of Bedlam,
Jaws of the keeper's world and that odd blend
Of machines and apology and pride.

Inside is movement, arbitrary as ants',
Where children with their immoderate gestures
Put yesterday's pecking orders to the test,
While unknown to themselves they store on file
Memories programmed like dragons' teeth.

Gatling, Vickers-Armstrong, Supermarine:
The notices instruct us not to touch,
For fear our fingers might be sensitized
By the thin glaze of suffering and animus
That coats all this armourers' stock-in-trade.

The sun aims sideways, under and beyond
The strong-arm stuff of the fifteen-inch guns,
And, against the fumes of the Lambeth Road,
Shows spots of pink and yellow where absent-minded
Roses have gone to sleep with their lights burning.

HAMPTON COURT
From *The Rape of the Lock*

Close by those meads, for ever crown'd with flow'rs,
Where Thames with pride surveys his rising tow'rs,
There stands a structure of majestic frame,
Which from the neighb'ring Hampton takes its name.
Here Britain's statesmen oft the fall foredoom
Of foreign tyrants, and of nymphs at home;
Here thou, great ANNA! whom three realms obey,
Dost sometimes counsel take – and sometimes Tea.

Hither the heroes and the nymphs resort,
To taste awhile the pleasures of a Court;
In various talk th' instructive hours they past,
Who gave the ball, or paid the visit last;
One speaks the glory of the British Queen,
And one describes a charming Indian screen;
A third interprets motions, looks, and eyes;
At ev'ry word a reputation dies.
Snuff, or the fan, supply each pause of chat,
With singing, laughing, ogling, and all that.

Mean while, declining from the noon of day,
The sun obliquely shoots his burning ray;
The hungry Judges soon the sentence sign,
And wretches hang that jury-men may dine;
The merchant from th'Exchange returns in peace,
And the long labours of the Toilet cease.
[. .]

ALEXANDER POPE (1688–1744)   139

A SPELLBOUND PALACE
(*Hampton Court*)

On this kindly yellow day of mild low-travelling
    winter sun
        The stirless depths of the yews
        Are vague with misty blues:
Across the spacious pathways stretching spires of
    shadow run,
And the wind-gnawed walls of ancient brick are fired
    vermilion.

        Two or three early sanguine finches tune
        Some tentative strains, to be enlarged by May
        or June:
           From a thrush or blackbird
           Comes now and then a word,
While an enfeebled fountain somewhere within is
    heard.

           Our footsteps wait awhile,
           Then draw beneath the pile,
           When an inner court outspreads
           As 'twere History's own asile,
Where the now-visioned fountain its attenuate crystal
    sheds

In passive lapse that seems to ignore the yon world's
    clamorous clutch,
And lays an insistent numbness on the place, like a
    cold hand's touch.

And there swaggers the Shade of a straddling King,
    plumed, sworded, with sensual face,
And lo, too, that of his Minister, at a bold self-centred
    pace:
Sheer in the sun they pass: and thereupon all is still,
Save the mindless fountain tinkling on with thin
    enfeebled will.

TWICKENHAM GARDEN

Blasted with sighs, and surrounded with tears,
 Hither I come to seek the spring,
 And at mine eyes, and at mine ears,
Receive such balms, as else cure everything;
 But O, self-traitor, I do bring
The spider love, which transubstantiates all,
 And can convert Manna to gall,
And that this place may thoroughly be thought
 True Paradise, I have the serpent brought.

'Twere wholesomer for me, that winter did
 Benight the glory of this place,
 And that a grave frost did forbid
These trees to laugh, and mock me to my face;
 But that I may not this disgrace
Endure, nor yet leave loving, Love, let me
 Some senseless piece of this place be:
Make me a mandrake, so I may groan here,
 Or a stone fountain weeping out my year.

Hither with crystal vials, lovers come,
 And take my tears, which are love's wine,
 And try your mistress' tears at home,
For all are false, that taste not just like mine;
 Alas, hearts do not in eyes shine,

Nor can you more judge woman's thoughts by tears,
  Than by her shadow, what she wears.
O perverse sex, where none is true but she,
  Who's therefore true, because her truth kills me.

JOHN DONNE (1572–1631)

PROLOGUE TO *HENRY V*

O for a Muse of fire, that would ascend
The brightest heaven of invention,
A kingdom for a stage, princes to act
And monarchs to behold the swelling scene!
Then should the warlike Harry, like himself,
Assume the port of Mars; and at his heels,
Leash'd in like hounds, should famine, sword and fire
Crouch for employment. But pardon, and gentles all,
The flat unraised spirits that have dared
On this unworthy scaffold to bring forth
So great an object: can this cockpit hold
The vasty fields of France? or may we cram
Within this wooden O the very casques
That did affright the air at Agincourt?
O, pardon! since a crooked figure may
Attest in little place a million;
And let us, ciphers to this great accompt,
On your imaginary forces work.
Suppose within the girdle of these walls
Are now confined two mighty monarchies,
Whose high upreared and abutting fronts
The perilous narrow ocean parts asunder:
Piece out our imperfections with your thoughts;
Into a thousand parts divide one man,
And make imaginary puissance;

Think, when we talk of horses, that you see them
Printing their proud hoofs i' th' receiving earth;
For 'tis your thoughts that now must deck our kings,
Carry them here and there; jumping o'er times,
Turning th' accomplishment of many years
Into an hour-glass: for the which supply,
Admit me Chorus to this history;
Who Prologue-like your humble patience pray,
Gently to hear, kindly to judge, our play.

From ON THE DEATH OF THE FAMOUS ACTOR, RICHARD BURBAGE

He's gone, and with him what a world are dead,
Friends, every one, and what a blank instead!
Take him for all in all, he was a man
Not to be match'd, and no age ever can.
No more young Hamlet, though but scant of breath,
Shall cry 'Revenge!' for his dear father's death.
Poor Romeo never more shall tears beget
For Juliet's love and cruel Capulet:
Harry shall not be seen as king or prince,
They died with thee, dear Dick [. .]

Tyrant Macbeth, with unwash'd, bloody hand,
We vainly now may hope to understand.
Brutus and Marcius henceforth must be dumb,
For ne'er thy like upon the stage shall come,
To charm the faculty of ears and eyes,
Unless we could command the dead to rise.
Vindex is gone, and what a loss was he!
Frankford, Brachiano, and Malevole,
Heart-broke Philaster, and Amintas too,
Are lost for ever; with the red-hair'd Jew,
Which sought the bankrupt merchant's pound of flesh,
By woman-lawyer caught in his own mesh.
What a wide world was in that little space,

Thyself a world the Globe thy fittest place!
Thy stature small, but every thought and mood
Might throughly from thy face be understood;
And his whole action he could change with ease
From ancient Lear to youthful Pericles.
But let me not forget one chiefest part,
Wherein, beyond the rest, he mov'd the heart;
The grieved Moor, made jealous by a slave,
Who sent his wife to fill a timeless grave,
Then slew himself upon the bloody bed.
All these and many more are with him dead.
Hereafter must our Poets cease to write.
Since thou art gone, dear Dick, a tragic night
Will wrap our black-hung stage: he made a Poet,
And those who yet remain full surely know it,
For, having Burbage to give forth each line,
It fill'd their brain with fury more divine.
Oft have I seen him leap into the grave,
Suiting the person, which he seem'd to have,
Of a mad lover, with so true an eye,
That there I would have sworn he meant to die.
[.]

ON SALATHIEL PAVY: A CHILD OF QUEEN ELIZABETH'S CHAPEL

Weep with me, all you that read
   This little story;
And know, for whom a tear you shed
   Death's self is sorry.
'Twas a child that so did thrive
   In grace and feature,
As Heaven and Nature seem'd to strive
   Which own'd the creature.
Years he number'd scarce thirteen
   When Fates turn'd cruel,
Yet three fill'd zodiacs had he been
   The stage's jewel;
And did act (what now we moan)
   Old men so duly,
As sooth the Parcae thought him one,
   He play'd so truly.
So, by error, to his fate
   They all consented;
But, viewing him since, alas! too late,
   They have relented;
And have sought, to give new birth,
   In baths to steep him;
But, being so much too good for earth,
   Heaven vows to keep him.

From TO THE MEMORY OF
MY BELOVED, THE AUTHOR,
MR. WILLIAM SHAKESPEARE

[. .] My Shakespeare, rise! I will not lodge thee by
Chaucer, or Spenser, or bid Beaumont lie
A little further, to make thee a room:
Thou art a monument without a tomb,
And art alive still while thy book doth live
And we have wits to read and praise to give.
That I not mix thee so, my brain excuses,
I mean with great, but disproportion'd Muses,
For if I thought my judgment were of years,
I should commit thee surely with thy peers,
And tell how far thou didst our Lyly outshine,
Or sporting Kyd, or Marlowe's mighty line.
And though thou hadst small Latin and less Greek,
From thence to honour thee, I would not seek
For names; but call forth thund'ring Aeschylus,
Euripides and Sophocles to us [. .]

Sweet Swan of Avon! what a sight it were
To see thee in our waters yet appear,
And make those flights upon the banks of Thames,
That so did take Eliza and our James!
But stay, I see thee in the hemisphere
Advanc'd, and made a constellation there!

Shine forth, thou star of poets, and with rage
Or influence, chide or cheer the drooping stage;
Which, since thy flight from hence, hath mourn'd like
    night,
And despairs day, but for thy volume's light.

DAY AND NIGHT

DAY AND NIGHT

LONDON'S SUMMER MORNING

Who has not waked to list the busy sounds
Of summer's morning, in the sultry smoke
Of noisy London? On the pavement hot
The sooty chimney-boy, with dingy face
And tattered covering, shrilly bawls his trade,
Rousing the sleepy housemaid. At the door
The milk-pail rattles, and the tinkling bell
Proclaims the dustman's office; while the street
Is lost in clouds impervious. Now begins
The din of hackney-coaches, waggons, carts;
While tinmen's shops, and noisy trunk-makers,
Knife-grinders, coopers, squeaking cork-cutters,
Fruit-barrows, and the hunger-giving cries
Of vegetable-vendors, fill the air.
Now every shop displays its varied trade,
And the fresh-sprinkled pavement cools the feet
Of early walkers. At the private door
The ruddy housemaid twirls the busy mop,
Annoying the smart 'prentice, or neat girl,
Tripping with band-box lightly. Now the sun
Darts burning splendour on the glittering pane,
Save where the canvas awning throws a shade
On the gay merchandise. Now, spruce and trim,
In shops (where beauty smiles with industry)
Sits the smart damsel; while the passenger

Peeps through the window, watching every charm.
Now pastry dainties catch the eye minute
Of humming insects, while the limy snare
Waits to enthrall them. Now the lamp-lighter
Mounts the tall ladder, nimbly venturous,
To trim the half-filled lamps, while at his feet
The pot-boy yells discordant! All along
The sultry pavement, the old-clothes-man cries
In tone monotonous, while sidelong views
The area for his traffic: now the bag
Is slyly opened, and the half-worn suit
(Sometimes the pilfered treasure of the base
Domestic spoiler), for one half its worth,
Sinks in the green abyss. The porter now
Bears his huge load along the burning way;
And the poor poet wakes from busy dreams,
To paint the summer morning.

LONDON DAWN

Dawn comes up on London
And night's undone.
Stars are routed
And street lamps outed,
Sodden great clouds begin to sail again
Like all-night anchored galleons to the main
From careful shallows to the far-withdrawn
Wide outer seas of sky.
Sleepers above river change their pain,
Lockhart's shows lively up Blackfriars Lane.
Motors dash by
With 'Mirrors', 'Mails', 'Telegraphs', what not?
South shore of Thames on London shows a blot
And first careful coffee-stall is withdrawn.
Only the poet strolls about at ease
Wondering what mortal thing his soul may please,
And spitting at the drains, while Paul's as ever
Is mighty and a king of sky and river,
And cares no more, Much-Father, for this one
Broke child, although a poet-born and clever,
Than any spit-kid of seven million
Must drudge all day until his earning's done.
A huffler has her red sails just a-quiver;
Sun's very near now and the tide's a-run.

IVOR GURNEY (1890–1937)   155

AUBADE 1940

Low behind Battersea power-station the dawn sags,
Dipping shafts of madder in a pearl pool.
Across the roofs a dogtail of smoke scampers and wags.

A sentry at the barracks renovates his nail
With bayonet-point, stamps hard to thaw his legs,
Wanting relief, and breakfast, and the mail.

Up from the shelters a new day returns.
Past crestfallen houses and bomb-shuffled slates
Workers kick shrapnel off the paving-stones.

And the whole city opens with a shout.
Hatred's more fierce the fiercer London burns.
The fires their last night's bombing lit are out.

In Bermondsey and Bow the fires are out; the water
That hissed with melted sugar, has been calmed.
And Peace sits spinning like Pohjola's daughter

Virginal on a rainbow. Suspended above doom
On stalks of hope, the barrage-balloons shine bright
Like a hundred shuttles waiting in the loom.

156   GEOFFREY MATTHEWS (1920–84)

BUSINESS GIRLS

From the geyser ventilators
  Autumn winds are blowing down
On a thousand business women
  Having baths in Camden Town.

Waste pipes chuckle into runnels,
  Steam's escaping here and there,
Morning trains through Camden cutting
  Shake the Crescent and the Square.

Early nip of changeful autumn,
  Dahlias glimpsed through garden doors,
At the back precarious bathrooms
  Jutting out from upper floors;

And behind their frail partitions
  Business women lie and soak,
Seeing through the draughty skylight
  Flying clouds and railway smoke.

Rest you there, poor unbelov'd ones,
  Lap your loneliness in heat.
All too soon the tiny breakfast,
  Trolley-bus and windy street.

SIR JOHN BETJEMAN (1906–84)   157

THE REAL SCENE
From *The Prelude: Book VII*

And now I look'd upon the real scene,
Familiarly perused it day by day
With keen and lively pleasure even there
Where disappointment was the strongest, pleased
Through courteous self-submission, as a tax
Paid to the object by prescriptive right,
A thing that ought to be. Shall I give way,
Copying the impression of the memory,
Though things remembered idly do half seem
The work of Fancy, shall I, as the mood
Inclines me, here describe, for pastime's sake,
Some portion of that motley imagery,
A vivid picture of my youth, and now
Among the lonely places that I love
A frequent day-dream for my riper mind?
– And first the look and aspect of the place:
The broad high-way appearance, as it strikes
On Strangers of all ages, the quick dance
Of colours, lights and forms, the Babel din,
The endless stream of men, and moving things,
From hour to hour the illimitable walk
Still among streets with clouds and sky above,
The wealth, the bustle and the eagerness,
The glittering Chariots with their pamper'd Steeds,

Stalls, Barrows, Porters; midway in the Street
The Scavenger, who begs with hat in hand,
The labouring Hackney Coaches, the rash speed
Of Coaches travelling far, whirl'd on with horn
Loud blowing, and the sturdy Drayman's Team,
Ascending from some Alley of the Thames
And striking right across the crowded Strand
Till the fore Horse veer round with punctual skill:
Here, there and everywhere a weary throng,
The Comers and the Goers face to face,
Face after face; the string of dazzling Wares,
Shop after shop, with Symbols, blazon'd Names,
And all the Tradesman's honours overhead;
Here, fronts of houses, like a title-page
With letters huge inscribed from top to toe;
Station'd above the door, like guardian Saints,
There, allegoric shapes, female or male;
Or physiognomies of real men,
Land-Warriors, Kings, or Admirals of the Sea,
Boyle, Shakespear, Newton, or the attractive head
Of some Scotch doctor, famous in his day.

   Meanwhile the roar continues, till at length,
Escaped as from an enemy, we turn
Abruptly into some sequester'd nook
Still as a shelter'd place when winds blow loud:
At leisure thence, through tracts of thin resort,

And sights and sounds that come at intervals,
We take our way; a raree-show is here
With Children gather'd round, another Street
Presents a company of dancing Dogs,
Or Dromedary, with an antic pair
Of Monkies on his back, a minstrel Band
Of Savoyards, or, single and alone,
An English Ballad-singer. Private Courts,
Gloomy as Coffins, and unsightly Lanes
Thrill'd by some female Vender's scream, belike
The very shrillest of all London Cries,
May then entangle us a while,
Conducted through these labyrinths unawares
To privileg'd Regions and inviolate,
Where from their airy lodges studious Lawyers
Look out on waters, walks, and gardens green.

THE BLIND BEGGAR
From *The Prelude, Book VII*

How often in the overflowing Streets,
Have I gone forward with the Crowd, and said
Unto myself, the face of every one
That passes by me is a mystery.
Thus have I look'd, nor ceas'd to look, oppress'd
By thoughts of what, and whither, when and how,
Until the shapes before my eyes became
A second-sight procession, such as glides
Over still mountains, or appears in dreams;
And all the ballast of familiar life,
The present, and the past; hope, fear; all stays,
All laws of acting, thinking, speaking man,
Went from me, neither knowing me, nor known.
And once, far-travell'd in such mood, beyond
The reach of common indications, lost
Amid the moving pageant, 'twas my chance
Abruptly to be smitten with the view
Of a blind Beggar, who, with upright face,
Stood propp'd against a Wall, upon his Chest
Wearing a written paper, to explain
The story of the Man, and who he was.
My mind did at this spectacle turn round
As with the might of waters, and it seemed
To me that in this Label was a type,

Or emblem, of the utmost that we know,
Both of ourselves and of the universe;
And, on the shape of the unmoving man,
His fixèd face and sightless eyes, I look'd
As if admonish'd from another world.

A DESCRIPTION OF A CITY SHOWER

Careful Observers may fortel the Hour
(By sure Prognosticks) when to dread a Show'r:
While Rain depends, the pensive Cat gives o'er
Her Frolicks, and pursues her Tail no more.
Returning Home at Night, you'll find the Sink
Strike your offended Sense with double Stink.
If you be wise, then go not far to Dine,
You spend in Coach-hire more than save in Wine,
A coming Show'r your shooting Corns presage,
Old Aches throb, your hollow Tooth will rage.
Sauntring in Coffee-house is *Dulman* seen;
He damns the Climate, and complains of Spleen.

Mean while the South, rising with dabbled Wings,
A Sable Cloud a-thwart the Welkin flings,
That swill'd more Liquor than it could contain,
And, like a Drunkard, gives it up again.
Brisk *Susan* whips her Linen from the Rope,
While the first drizzling Show'r is born aslope,
Such is that Sprinkling which some careless Quean
Flirts on you from her Mop, but not so clean.
You fly, invoke the Gods; then turning, stop
To rail; she singing, still whirls on her Mop.
Not yet, the Dust had shun'd th' unequal Strife,
But aided by the Wind, fought still for Life;

And wafted with its Foe by violent Gust,
'Twas doubtful which was Rain, and which was Dust.
Ah! where must needy Poet seek for Aid,
When Dust and Rain at once his Coat invade;
Sole Coat, where Dust cemented by the Rain,
Erects the Nap, and leaves a cloudy Stain.

Now in contiguous Drops the Flood comes down,
Threat'ning with Deluge this *Devoted* Town.
To Shops in Crouds the dagled Females fly,
Pretend to cheapen Goods, but nothing buy.
The Templer spruce, while ev'ry Spout's a-broach,
Stays till 'tis fair, yet seems to call a Coach.
The tuck'd-up Sempstress walks with hasty Strides,
While Streams run down her oil'd Umbrella's Sides.
Here various Kinds by various Fortunes led,
Commence Acquaintance underneath a Shed.
Triumphant Tories, and desponding Whigs,
Forget their Fewds, and join to save their Wigs.
Box'd in a Chair the Beau impatient sits,
While Spouts run clatt'ring o'er the Roof by Fits;
And ever and anon with frightful Din
The Leather sounds, he trembles from within.
So when *Troy* Chair-men bore the Wooden Steed,
Pregnant with *Greeks*, impatient to be freed,
(Those Bully *Greeks*, who, as the Moderns do,
Instead of paying Chair-men, run them thro'.)

Laoco'n struck the Outside with his Spear,
And each imprison'd Hero quak'd for Fear.

   Now from all Parts the swelling Kennels flow,
And bear their Trophies with them as they go:
Filth of all Hues and Odours seem to tell
What Streets they sail'd from, by the Sight and Smell.
They, as each Torrent drives, with rapid Force
From *Smithfield*, or St. *Pulchre's* shape their Course,
And in huge Confluent join at *Snow-Hill* Ridge,
Fall from the *Conduit* prone to *Holborn-Bridge.*
Sweepings from Butchers Stalls, Dung, Guts, and
    Blood,
Drown'd Puppies, stinking Sprats, all drench'd in Mud,
Dead Cats, and Turnip-Tops, come tumbling down
    the Flood.

JONATHAN SWIFT (1667–1745)   165

FOG
From *The Feast of St. Hilary*

I love the fog: in every street
   Shrill muffled cries and shapes forlorn,
The frosted hoof with stealthy beat,
   The hollow-sounding motor-horn:

A fog that lasts till, gently wrung
   By Pythian pangs, we realize
That Doomsday somewhere dawns among
   The systems and the galaxies,

And ruin at the swiftest rate
   The chartered destinies pursue;
While as for us, our final fate
   Already fixed with small ado,

Spills on our heads no wrathful cup,
   Nor wrecks us on a fiery shore,
But leaves us simply swallowed up
   In London fog for evermore.

PICK-POCKETS
From *Trivia*

Where the mob gathers, swiftly shoot along,
Nor idly mingle in the noisy throng.
Lur'd by the silver hilt, amid the swarm,
The subtil artist will thy side disarm.
Nor is thy flaxen wigg with safety worn;
High on the shoulder, in the basket born,
Lurks the sly boy, whose hand to rapine bred,
Plucks off the curling honours of thy head.
Here dives the skulking thief, with practis'd slight,
And unfelt fingers make thy pocket light.
Where's now thy watch, with all its trinkets, flown?
And thy late snuff-box is no more thy own.
But lo! his bolder theft some tradesman spies,
Swift from his prey the scudding lurcher flies;
Dext'rous he 'scapes the coach, with nimble bounds,
While ev'ry honest tongue *Stop Thief* resounds.
So speeds the wily fox, alarm'd by fear,
Who lately filch'd the turkey's callow care;
Hounds following hounds grow louder as he flies,
And injur'd tenants joyn the hunter's cries.
Breathless he stumbling falls: ill-fated boy!
Why did not honest work thy youth employ?

Seiz'd by rough hands, he's dragg'd amid the rout,
And stretch'd beneath the pump's incessant spout:
Or plung'd in miry ponds, he gasping lies,
Mud choakes his mouth, and plasters o'er his eyes.

AN OLD-FASHIONED TRAVELLER ON
THE TRADE ROUTES

I was sitting upstairs in a bus, cursing the waste of time, and pouring my life away on one of those insane journeys across London – while gradually the wavering motion of this precarious glass salon, that flung us about softly like trusses of wheat or Judo Lords, began its medicinal work inside the magnetic landscape of London.

The bus, with its transparent decks of people, trembled. And was as uniquely ceremonious in propelling itself as an eminent Jellyfish with an iron will, by expulsions, valves, hisses, steams, and emotional respirations. A militant, elementary, caparisoned Jellyfish, of the feminine sex, systematically eating and drinking the sea.

I began to feel as battered as though I had been making love all night! My limbs distilled the same interesting wide-awake weariness.

We went forward at a swimmer's pace, gazing through the walls that rocked the weather about like a cloudy drink from a chemist's shop – with the depth and sting of the Baltic. The air-shocks, the sulphur dioxides, the gelatin ignitions! We were all of us parcelled up in mud-coloured clothes, dreaming, while the rich perishable ensemble – as stuffy and exclusive as a bag of fish and chips, or as an Eskimo's bed in a glass drift – cautiously advanced as though on an exercise from a naval college.

The jogging was so consistently idiotic, it induced a feeling of complete security. I gave up my complicated life on the spot; and lay screwed up like an old handkerchief screwed up in a pocket, suspended in time, ready to go to the ends of the earth. O trans-Siberian railways! Balloons! Astronauts!

BUSES ON THE STRAND

The Strand is beautiful with buses,
    Fat and majestical in form,
Red like tomatoes in their trusses
    In August, when the sun is warm.

They cluster in the builded chasm,
    Corpulent fruit, a hundred strong,
And now and then a secret spasm
    Spurs them a yard or two along.

Scarlet and portly and seraphic,
    Contented in the summer's prime,
They beam among the jumbled traffic,
    Patiently ripening with time,

Till, with a final jerk and rumble,
    The Strand tomatoes, fat and fair,
Roll past the traffic lights and tumble
    Gleefully down Trafalgar Square.

R. P. LISTER (1914–2014)

TO A DISUSED PHONE BOX

When was the last time I stepped inside?
The directory has gone, so too
the operator who once upon a time
would connect the wires and put us through.
Haven now of the rootless or the robbed,
resort of those who leave no trace except
grease and sweat on the handle,
breath snared in the mouthpiece's mesh.
Yet you still invite this devotion:
to arrange each piece of silver on the ledge
then dial from memory, listening for the release,
the plummet into your collection.
The tone is as warm as blood, my own.
Someone picks up. *Who's there?*
It's the boy crouched beneath the stairs,
waiting for a word to travel along
the piece of string stretched taut
between this receiver
and the can cupped to his ear.

RED LION, DUKE OF YORK STREET

From *Nairn's London*

If I could keep only one pub out of the whole London galaxy, this would be my choice. It is not especially comfortable or especially atmospheric, but it strikes deeper than any other. All around the walls are magnificent cut-glass mirrors, the best in London, recently renovated so that they gleam as sharply as they ever did. And, as the bar space is roughly square, wall after wall after wall is reflected in the real walls, a process which oddly enough reinforces the solidity. Nothing is fuzzy, but everything has incredible depth and compassion combined with brilliance. It is the spirit exactly of Manet's *Bar at the Folies Bergère*. It sees and feels everything, yet you are thrown back on your own resources, enriched. This is the opposite thing to the gentle, sentimental pub where you can wash your troubles into oblivion. If you had a problem, the Red Lion could not ease *it*, however much you drank; instead it would strengthen *you*. It is a place to walk out of ramrod-straight, reinforced by those proud, sparkling arabesques.

IAN NAIRN (1930–83)   173

LAMENT FOR 'THE OLD SWAN',
NOTTING HILL GATE

The Old Swan has gone. They have widened the road.
A year ago they closed her, and she stood,
The neighbouring houses pulled down, suddenly
    revealed
In all her touching pretentiousness
Of turret and Gothic pinnacle, like
A stupid and ugly woman
Unexpectedly struck to dignity by bereavement.

And now she has vanished. The gap elicits
A guarded sentiment. Enough bad poets
Have romanticized beer and pubs,
And those for whom the gimcrack enchantments
Of engraved glass, mahogany, plants in pots,
Were all laid out to please, are fugitives, doubtless,
Nightly self-immersed in a fake splendour.

Yet a Public House perhaps makes manifest also
The hidden City; implies its laws
Of tolerance, hierarchy, exchange.
Friends I remember there, enemies, acquaintances,
Some drabs and drunks, some bores and boors,
    and many

Indifferent and decent people. They will drink
    elsewhere.
Anonymous, it harboured
The dreadful, innocent martyrs
Of megalopolis – Christie or Heath.

Now that's finished with. And all the wide
And sober roads of the world walk sensibly onwards
Into the featureless future. But the white swans
That dipped and swam in each great lucid mirror
Remain in the mind only, remain as a lost symbol.

DON JUAN IN LONDON
From *Don Juan*

His morns he pass'd in business – which dissected,
    Was like all business, a laborious nothing,
That leads to lassitude, the most infected
    And Centaur Nessus garb of mortal clothing,
And on our sofas makes us lie dejected,
    And talk in tender horrors of our loathing
All kinds of toil, save for our country's good –
Which grows no better, though 'tis time it should.

His afternoons he pass'd in visits, luncheons,
    Lounging, and boxing; and the twilight hour
In riding round those vegetable puncheons
    Call'd 'Parks', where there is neither fruit nor
        flower
Enough to gratify a bee's slight munchings;
    But, after all, it is the only 'bower'
(In Moore's phrase) where the fashionable fair
Can form a slight acquaintance with fresh air.

Then dress, then dinner, then awakes the world!
    Then glare the lamps, then whirl the wheels, then
        roar
Through street and square fast flashing chariots hurl'd
    Like harness'd meteors; then along the floor

Chalk mimics painting; then festoons are twirl'd;
    Then roll the brazen thunders of the door,
Which opens to the thousand happy few,
An earthly paradise of *Or Molu*.

There stands the noble hostess, nor shall sink
    With the three thousandth curtsey; there the waltz,
The only dance which teaches girls to think,
    Makes one in love even with its very faults.
Salon, room, hall, o'erflow beyond their brink,
    And long the latest of arrivals halts,
'Midst royal dukes, and dames condemn'd to climb,
And gain an inch of staircase at a time.

Thrice happy he who, after a survey
    Of the good company, can win a corner,
A door that's *in*, or boudoir *out*, of the way,
    Where he can fix himself like small 'Jack Horner',
And let the Babel run round as it may,
    And look on as a mourner, or a scorner,
Or an approver, or a mere spectator,
    Yawning a little as the night grows later.

But this won't do, save by and by, and he
    Who, like Don Juan, takes an active share,
Must steer with care through all that glittering sea
    Of gems, and plumes, and pearls, and silks, to where

He deems it is his proper place to be:
   Dissolving in the waltz, to some soft air,
Or proudlier prancing, with mercurial skill,
   Where Science marshals forth her own quadrille.

Or, if he dance not, but hath higher views
   Upon an heiress or his neighbour's bride,
Let him take care that that which he pursues
   Is not at once too palpably descried.
Full many an eager gentleman oft rues
   His haste: impatience is a blundering guide,
Amongst a people famous for reflection,
Who like to play the fool with circumspection.

But if you can contrive, get next at supper;
   Or, if forestall'd, get opposite and ogle: –
Oh, ye ambrosial moments! always upper
   In mind, a sort of sentimental bogle,
Which sits for ever upon memory's crupper,
   The ghost of vanish'd pleasures once in vogue! Ill
Can tender souls relate the rise and fall
Of hopes and fears which shake a single ball.

A NOCTURNAL SKETCH

Even is come; and from the dark Park, hark,
The signal of the setting sun – one gun!
And six is sounding from the chime, prime time
To go and see the Drury-Lane Dane slain,
Or hear Othello's jealous doubt spout out,
Or Macbeth raving at that shade-made blade,
Denying to his frantic clutch much touch;
Or else to see Ducrow with wide stride ride
Four horses as no other man can span;
Or in the small Olympic pit, sit split
Laughing at Liston, while you quiz his phiz.

Anon Night comes, and with her wings brings things
Such as, with his poetic tongue, Young sung;
The gas upblazes with its bright white light,
And paralytic watchmen prowl, howl, growl
About the streets and take up Pall-Mall Sal,
Who, hasting to her nightly jobs, robs fobs.
Now thieves to enter for your cash, smash, crash,
Past drowsy Charley, in a deep sleep, creep,
But frightened by Policeman B 3, flee,
And while they're going, whisper low, 'No go!'

Now puss, while folks are in their beds, treads leads,
And sleepers waking grumble, 'Drat that cat!'

Who in the gutter caterwauls, squalls, mauls
Some feline foe, and screams in shrill ill-will.

Now Bulls of Bashan, of a prize size, rise
In childish dreams, and with a roar gore poor
Georgy, or Charley, or Billy, willy-nilly;
But nursemaid in a nightmare rest, chest-pressed,
Dreameth of one of her old flames, James Games,
And that she hears – what faith is man's! – Ann's banns
And his, from Reverend Mr. Rice, twice, thrice:
White ribbons flourish, and a stout shout out,
That upward goes, shows Rose knows those bows'
     woes!

A BALLAD OF LONDON

Ah, London! London! our delight,
Great flower that opens but at night,
Great City of the Midnight Sun,
Whose day begins when day is done.

Lamp after lamp against the sky
Opens a sudden beaming eye,
Leaping alight on either hand,
The iron lilies of the Strand.

Like dragonflies, the hansoms hover,
With jewelled eyes, to catch the lover;
The streets are full of lights and loves,
Soft gowns, and flutter of soiled doves.

The human moths about the light
Dash and cling close in dazed delight,
And burn and laugh, the world and wife,
For this is London, this is life!

Upon thy petals butterflies,
But at thy root, some say, there lies,
A world of weeping trodden things,
Poor worms that have not eyes or wings.

From out corruption of their woe
Springs this bright flower that charms us so,
Men die and rot deep out of sight
To keep this jungle-flower bright.

Paris and London, World-Flowers twain
Wherewith the World-Tree blooms again,
Since Time hath gathered Babylon,
And withered Rome still withers on.

Sidon and Tyre were such as ye,
How bright they shone upon the Tree!
But Time hath gathered, both are gone,
And no man sails to Babylon.

Ah, London! London! our delight,
For thee, too, the eternal night,
And Circe Paris hath no charm
To stay Time's unrelenting arm.

Time and his moths shall eat up all.
Your charming towers proud and tall
He shall most utterly abase,
And set a desert in their place.

THE EMBANKMENT

The fantasia of a fallen gentleman on a cold, bitter night.

Once, in finesse of fiddles found I ecstasy,
In the flash of gold heels on the hard pavement.
Now see I
That warmth's the very stuff of poesy.
Oh, God, make small
The old star-eaten blanket of the sky,
That I may fold it round me and in comfort lie.

T. E. HULME (1883–1917)   183

ONE SEEING AN OLD POET IN THE CAFÉ ROYAL

I saw him in the Café Royal,
    Very old and very grand.
Modernistic shone the lamplight
    There in London's fairyland.
'Devilled chicken. Devilled whitebait.
    Devil if I understand.

'Where is Oscar? Where is Bosie?
    Have I seen that man before?
And the old one in the corner,
    Is it really Wratislaw?'
Scent of Tutti-Frutti-Sen-Sen
    And cheroots upon the floor.

A NIGHTINGALE SANG IN
BERKELEY SQUARE

When two lovers meet in Mayfair, so the legends tell,
Songbirds sing and winter turns to spring.
Every winding street in Mayfair falls beneath
 the spell.
I know such enchantment can be,
'Cause it happened one evening to me:
That certain night, the night we met,
There was magic abroad in the air,
There were angels dining at the Ritz,
And a nightingale sang in Berkeley Square.

I may be right, I may be wrong,
But I'm perfectly willing to swear
That when you turned and smiled at me
A nightingale sang in Berkeley Square.

The moon that lingered over London town,
Poor puzzled moon, he wore a frown.
How could he know we two were so in love?
The whole darn world seemed upside down,
The streets of town were paved with stars;
It was such a romantic affair.
And, as we kissed and said 'goodnight',
A nightingale sang in Berkeley Square.

When dawn came stealing up all gold and blue
To interrupt our rendezvous,
I still remember how you smiled and said,
'Was that a dream or was it true?'
Our homeward step was just as light
As the tap-dancing feet of Astaire,
And, like an echo far away,
A nightingale sang in Berkeley Square.
I know 'cause I was there,
That night in Berkeley Square.

BEHIND THE SCENES: EMPIRE

The little painted angels flit,
See, down the narrow staircase, where
The pink legs flicker over it!

Blonde, and bewigged, and winged with gold,
The shining creatures of the air
Troop sadly, shivering with cold.

The gusty gaslight shoots a thin
Sharp finger over cheeks and nose
Rouged to the colour of the rose.

All wigs and paint, they hurry in:
Then, bid their radiant moment be
The footlights' immortality!

ARTHUR SYMONS (1865–1945)

ORPHEUS IN SOHO

His search is desperate!
And the little night-shops of the Underworld
With their kiosks . . . they know it,
The little bars as full of dust as a stale cake,
None of these places would exist without Orpheus
And how well they know it.

. . . when the word goes ahead to the next city,
An underworld is hastily constructed,
With bitch-clubs, with cellars and passages,
So that he can go on searching, desperately!

As the brim of the world is lit,
And breath pours softly over the Earth,
And as Heaven moves ahead to the next city
With deep airs, and with lights and rains,

He plunges into Hades, for his search is desperate!
And there is so little risk . . . down there,
That is the benefit of searching frenziedly
Among the dust-shops and blind-alleys
. . . there is so little risk of finding her
In Europe's old blue Kasbah, and he knows it.

From SOHO

Oh my Soho, my omphalos is your plague-pit of cross-
     rail diggings, the bleach-
stink of your newly rinsed tarmac, your 2for1 WKD
     deals,
your tatty rainbow flags, your porn shops, your
     cottages!
Warren's cup transforms from dirty secret to prize
     exhibit but I

am like you my Soho. I'm chock-full of shame, riven
     with dark man-
jostling alleyways, a treasure map of buried trauma.
     In you
I have spent my life – drunk, poppered up, tarnished,
     tear-stained, corroded, Eros-
like. Oh my Soho, unfurl the chiselled leaves of my
     fruit

family tree. Give me my batty-birth rite. Baptise me
     with pigeon
shit, cheap lager, cum. Oh my Soho, my urinal'd
utopia, my Mary-Jerusalem, my homo-land – may
     I call you my
daddy? You teach this queer continuation on the
     breaking

wheel of pansy progress so I still take my body into
    dungeons, cubicles, alleyways –
flesh to the grindstone – my only weapon against
    normativity! Oh my Soho,
your hunting cry rallies within my hot-pink veins.
    Familial
voice calling us home to reseed History.

From A SATIRE, IN IMITATION OF THE THIRD OF JUVENAL

'Here want of rest a-nights more people kills
Than all the college, and the weekly bills:
Where none have privilege to sleep, but those
Whose purses can compound for their repose:
In vain I go to bed, or close my eyes,
Methinks the place the middle region is,
Where I lie down in storms, in thunder rise:
The restless bells such din in steeples keep,
That scarce the dead can in their churchyards sleep:
Huzzas of drunkards, bellmen's midnight rhymes,
The noise of shops, with hawkers' early screams,
Besides the brawls of coachmen, when they meet,
And stop in turnings of a narrow street,
Such a loud medley of confusion make,
As drowsy Archer on the Bench would wake.
[. .]
   'If what I've said can't from the town affright,
Consider other dangers of the night:
When brickbats are from upper stories thrown,
And emptied chamber-pots come pouring down
From garret windows: you have cause to bless
The gentle stars, if you come off with piss:

So many fates attend, a man had need
Ne'er walk without a surgeon by his side,
And he can hardly now discreet be thought,
That does not make his will ere he go out.'

THE HAUNTED CITY
From *The Ghost*

Whilst Curiosity, whose rage
No mercy shows to sex or age,
Must be indulged at the expense
Of judgment, truth, and common sense,
Impostures cannot but prevail;
And when old miracles grow stale,
Jugglers will still the art pursue,
And entertain the world with new.
For them, obedient to their will,
And trembling at their mighty skill,
Sad spirits, summon'd from the tomb,
Glide, glaring ghastly, through the gloom;
In all the usual pomp of storms,
In horrid customary forms,
A wolf, a bear, a horse, an ape,
As Fear and Fancy give them shape,
Tormented with despair and pain,
They roar, they yell, and clank the chain.
Folly and Guilt (for Guilt, howe'er
The face of Courage it may wear,
Is still a coward at the heart)
At fear-created phantoms start.
The priest – that very word implies
That he's both innocent and wise –

Yet fears to travel in the dark,
Unless escorted by his clerk.
But let not every bungler deem
Too lightly of so deep a scheme;
For reputation of the art,
Each ghost must act a proper part,
Observe Decorum's needful grace,
And keep the laws of Time and Place;
Must change, with happy variation,
His manners with his situation;
What in the country might pass down,
Would be impertinent in town.
No spirit of discretion here
Can think of breeding awe and fear;
'Twill serve the purpose more by half
To make the congregation laugh.
We want no ensigns of surprise,
Locks stiff with gore, and saucer eyes;
Give us an entertaining sprite,
Gentle, familiar, and polite,
One who appears in such a form
As might an holy hermit warm,
Or who on former schemes refines,
And only talks by sounds and signs,
Who will not to the eye appear,
But pays her visits to the ear,
And knocks so gently, 't would not fright

A lady in the darkest night.
Such is our Fanny, whose good-will,
Which cannot in the grave lie still,
Brings her on earth to entertain
Her friends and lovers in Cock-lane.

A LONDON THOROUGHFARE, 2 A.M.

They have watered the street,
It shines in the glare of lamps,
Cold, white lamps,
And lies
Like a slow-moving river,
Barred with silver and black.
Cabs go down it,
One,
Then another.
Between them I hear the shuffling of feet.
Tramps doze on the window-ledges,
Night-walkers pass along the sidewalks.
The city is squalid and sinister,
With the silver-barred street in the midst,
Slow-moving,
A river leading nowhere.

Opposite my window,
The moon cuts,
Clear and round,
Through the plum-coloured night.
She cannot light the city;
It is too bright.
It has white lamps,
And glitters coldly.

I stand in the window and watch the moon.
She is thin and lustreless,
But I love her.
I know the moon,
And this is an alien city.

AMY LOWELL (1874–1925)

PARLIAMENT HILL IN THE EVENING

The houses fade in a melt of mist
    Blotching the thick, soiled air
With reddish places that still resist
    The Night's slow care.

The hopeless, wintry twilight fades,
    The city corrodes out of sight
As the body corrodes when death invades
    That citadel of delight.

Now verdigris smoulderings softly spread
    Through the shroud of the town, as slow
Night-lights hither and thither shed
    Their ghastly glow.

THE WORLD IN THE EVENING

It is a good time to watch the sky.
The clouds
Are not ordinary. They are apricot
Or prussian-blue,
Not vague at all.

Because the sun is setting now
Its obscurations become bright
And look quite solid.

While in the shadow-fall down here
The eroding high-rise flats
Someone imagined for the poor
Are changed as well
To cubic constellations:
As lights are switched on, one by one.

HUBERT WITHEFORD (1921–2000)

QUIET NEIGHBOURS

Sitting alone at night
Careless of time,
From the house next door
I hear the clock chime.

Ten, eleven, twelve;
One, two, three –
It is all the same to the clock,
And much the same to me.

But to-night more than sense heard it:
I opened my eyes wide
To look at the wall and wonder
What lay on the other side.

They are quiet people
That live next door;
I never hear them scrape
Their chairs along the floor,

They do not laugh loud, or sing,
Or scratch in the grate,
I have never seen a taxi
Drawn up at their gate;

And though their back-garden
Is always neat and trim
It has a humbled look
And no one walks therein.

So did not their chiming clock
Imply some hand to wind it,
I might doubt if the wall between us
Had any life behind it.

London neighbours are such
That I may never know more
Than this of the people
Who live next door.

While they for their part
Should they hazard a guess
At me on my side of the wall
Will know as little, or less;

For my life has grown quiet,
As quiet as theirs;
And the clock has been silent on my chimney-piece
For years and years.

SYLVIA TOWNSEND WARNER (1893–1978)   201

REGENT'S PARK TERRACE

The noises round my house. On cobbles bounding
Victorian-fashioned drays laden with railway goods;
their hollow sound like stones in rolling barrels:
the stony hoofing of dray horses.

Further, the trains themselves; among them the violent,
screaming like frightened animals, clashing metal;
different the pompous, the heavy breathers, the
    aldermen,
or those again which speed with the declining
sadness of crying along the distant routes
knitting together weathers and dialects.

Between these noises the little teeth
of a London silence.

Finally the lions grumbling over the park,
angry in the night hours,
cavernous as though their throats were openings up
    from the earth:
hooves, luggage, engines, tumbrils, lions,
hollow noises, noises of travel, hourly these unpick
the bricks of a London terrace, make the ear
their road, and have their audience in whatever
hearing the heart or the deep of the belly owns.

202   BERNARD SPENCER (1909–63)

LONDON SNOW

When men were all asleep the snow came flying,
In large white flakes falling on the city brown,
Stealthily and perpetually settling and loosely lying,
    Hushing the latest traffic of the drowsy town;
Deadening, muffling, stifling its murmurs failing;
Lazily and incessantly floating down and down:
    Silently sifting and veiling road, roof and railing;
Hiding difference, making unevenness even,
Into angles and crevices softly drifting and sailing.
    All night it fell, and when full inches seven
It lay in the depth of its uncompacted lightness,
The clouds blew off from a high and frosty heaven;
    And all woke earlier for the unaccustomed
        brightness
Of the winter dawning, the strange unheavenly glare:
The eye marvelled – marvelled at the dazzling
        whiteness;
    The ear hearkened to the stillness of the solemn air;
No sound of wheel rumbling nor of foot falling,
And the busy morning cries came thin and spare.
    Then boys I heard, as they went to school, calling,
They gathered up the crystal manna to freeze
Their tongues with tasting, their hands with
    snowballing;
    Or rioted in a drift, plunging up to the knees;

Or peering up from under the white-mossed wonder,
'O look at the trees!' they cried, 'O look at the trees!'
  With lessened load a few carts creak and blunder,
Following along the white deserted way,
A country company long dispersed asunder:
  When now already the sun, in pale display
Standing by Paul's high dome, spread forth below
His sparkling beams, and awoke the stir of the day.
  For now doors open, and war is waged with the
      snow;
And trains of sombre men, past tale of number,
Tread long brown paths, as toward their toil they go:
  But even for them awhile no cares encumber
Their minds diverted; the daily word is unspoken,
The daily thoughts of labour and sorrow slumber
At the sight of the beauty that greets them, for the
      charm they have broken.

ONE OF THESE NIGHTS
for Fleur Fitzgerald

A pregnant moon of August
composes the rooftops'
unventilated slopes;
dispenses to the dust
its milky balm. A blue
gibbon blinks in the zoo.

Cashel and Angkor Wat
are not more ghostly than
London now, its squares
bone-pale in the moonlight,
its quiet thoroughfares
a sea of desolation.

The grime of an ephemeral
culture is swept clean
by that celestial hoover,
the refuse of an era
consumed like polythene
in its impartial glare.

A train trembles deep
in the earth; vagrants sleep
beside the revolving doors
of vast department stores
past whose alarm systems
the moonlight blandly streams.

A breeze-ruffled news-stand
headlines the dole queues,
the bleak no-longer-news
of racism and inflation –
straws in the rising wind
that heralds the cyclone.

It all happened before –
the road to Wigan Pier,
the long road from Jarrow
to the tea room at the Ritz;
Munich, the Phoney War,
the convoys and the Blitz.

One of these nights quiescent
sirens will start to go –
a dog howl reminiscent
of forty years ago –
and sleepy people file
down to the shelters while

radiant warplanes come
droning up the Thames from
Gravesend to Blackfriars,
Westminster and Mayfair,
their incandescent flowers
unfolding everywhere.

Enchanted foliage, bright
water as in an old film
in sumptuous black and white –
this is the true realm,
the real earth before
business and empire;
and life begins tonight.

GREENWICH OBSERVATORY

This onion-dome holds all intricacies
Of intellect and star-struck wisdom; so
Like Coleridge's head with multitudinous
Passages riddled, full of strange instruments
Unbalanced by a touch, this organism
From wires and dials spins introverted life.
It never looks, squat on its concrete shoulders,
Down at the river's swarming life, nor sees
Cranes' groping insect-like activity
Nor slow procession of funnels past the docks.
Turning its inner wheels, absorbed in problems
Of space and time, it never hears
Birds singing in the park or children's laughter.
Alive, but in another way, it broods
On this its Highgate, hypnotized
In lunar reverie and calculation.
Yet night awakes it; blind lids open
Leaden to look upon the moon:
A single goggling telescopic eye
Enfolds the spheric wonder of the sky.

NATURE AND PLACE

ODE TO A NIGHTINGALE

My heart aches, and a drowsy numbness pains
  My sense, as though of hemlock I had drunk,
Or emptied some dull opiate to the drains
  One minute past, and Lethe-wards had sunk:
'Tis not through envy of thy happy lot,
  But being too happy in thine happiness, –
    That thou, light-winged Dryad of the trees
      In some melodious plot
Of beechen green, and shadows numberless,
  Singest of summer in full-throated ease.

O, for a draught of vintage! that hath been
  Cool'd a long age in the deep-delved earth,
Tasting of Flora and the country green,
  Dance, and Provençal song, and sunburnt mirth!
O for a beaker full of the warm South,
  Full of the true, the blushful Hippocrene,
    With beaded bubbles winking at the brim,
      And purple-stained mouth;
  That I might drink, and leave the world unseen,
    And with thee fade away into the forest dim:

Fade far away, dissolve, and quite forget
  What thou among the leaves hast never known,
The weariness, the fever, and the fret

Here, where men sit and hear each other groan;
Where palsy shakes a few, sad, last gray hairs,
   Where youth grows pale, and spectre-thin, and
       dies;
     Where but to think is to be full of sorrow
      And leaden-eyed despairs,
   Where Beauty cannot keep her lustrous eyes,
    Or new Love pine at them beyond to-morrow.

Away! away! for I will fly to thee,
   Not charioted by Bacchus and his pards,
But on the viewless wings of Poesy,
   Though the dull brain perplexes and retards:
Already with thee! tender is the night,
   And haply the Queen-Moon is on her throne,
     Cluster'd around by all her starry Fays;
      But here there is no light,
   Save what from heaven is with the breezes blown
    Through verdurous glooms and winding mossy
      ways.

I cannot see what flowers are at my feet,
   Nor what soft incense hangs upon the boughs,
But, in embalmed darkness, guess each sweet
   Wherewith the seasonable month endows
The grass, the thicket, and the fruit-tree wild;
   White hawthorn, and the pastoral eglantine;

Fast fading violets cover'd up in leaves;
    And mid-May's eldest child,
The coming musk-rose, full of dewy wine,
    The murmurous haunt of flies on summer eves.

Darkling I listen; and, for many a time
    I have been half in love with easeful Death,
Call'd him soft names in many a mused rhyme,
    To take into the air my quiet breath;
      Now more than ever seems it rich to die,
    To cease upon the midnight with no pain,
      While thou art pouring forth thy soul abroad
        In such an ecstasy!
    Still wouldst thou sing, and I have ears in vain –
    To thy high requiem become a sod.

Thou wast not born for death, immortal Bird!
    No hungry generations tread thee down;
The voice I hear this passing night was heard
    In ancient days by emperor and clown:
Perhaps the self-same song that found a path
    Through the sad heart of Ruth, when, sick for
      home,
      She stood in tears amid the alien corn;
        The same that oft-times hath
Charm'd magic casements, opening on the foam
    Of perilous seas, in faery lands forlorn.

Forlorn! the very word is like a bell
　To toll me back from thee to my sole self!
Adieu! the fancy cannot cheat so well
　As she is fam'd to do, deceiving elf.
Adieu! adieu! thy plaintive anthem fades
　　Past the near meadows, over the still stream,
　　　Up the hill-side; and now 'tis buried deep
　　　　In the next valley-glades:
　Was it a vision, or a waking dream?
　　　Fled is that music: – Do I wake or sleep?

KEATS AT HIGHGATE

A cheerful youth joined Coleridge on his walk
('Loose,' noted Coleridge, 'slack, and not well-
    dressed')
Listening respectfully to the talk talk talk
Of First and Second Consciousness, then pressed
The famous hand with warmth and sauntered back
Homeward in his own state of less dispersed
More passive consciousness – passive, not slack,
Whether of Secondary type or First.

He made his way toward Hampstead so alert
He hardly passed the small grey ponds below
Or watched a sparrow pecking in the dirt
Without some insight swelling the mind's flow
That banks made swift. Everything put to use.
Perhaps not well-dressed but oh no not loose.

THOM GUNN (1929–2004)

A LONDON PLANE-TREE

Green is the plane-tree in the square,
    The other trees are brown;
They droop and pine for country air;
    The plane-tree loved the town.

Here from my garret-pane, I mark
    The plane-tree bud and blow,
Shed her recuperative bark,
    And spread her shade below.

Among her branches, in and out,
    The city breezes play;
The dun fog wraps her round about;
    Above, the smoke curls grey.

Others the country take for choice,
    And hold the town in scorn;
But she has listened to the voice
    On city breezes borne.

LETTER FROM TOWN:
THE ALMOND-TREE

You promised to send me some violets. Did you forget?
  White ones and blue ones from under the orchard
    hedge?
  Sweet dark purple, and white ones mixed for a
    pledge
Of our early love that hardly has opened yet.

Here there's an almond-tree – you have never seen
  Such a one in the north – it flowers on the street,
    and I stand
  Every day by the fence to look up at the flowers that
    expand
At rest in the blue, and wonder at what they mean.

Under the almond-tree, the happy lands
  Provence, Japan, and Italy repose;
  And passing feet are chatter and clapping of those
Who play around us, country girls clapping their hands.

You, my love, the foremost, in a flowered gown,
  All your unbearable tenderness, you with the
    laughter
  Startled upon your eyes now so wide with hereafter,
You with loose hands of abandonment hanging down.

D. H. LAWRENCE (1885–1930)

CLOSED SKY
From *Winter and London*

A hundred mornings greet the same closed sky,
one of nature's shows, one mantle wrapping
the dust of London with the dust of Europe –
in the interiors it is always night.
The clouds are welcome to us as insulation,
a silencer to the ultimate blue sky,
naked heaven's monologue with man.
In my country, the wettest Englishman
sparkles with approbation, magnifying
curious small things I could never see –
under closed sky, trifles are luminous,
gossip makes New York and London one,
one mouth . . . we use identical instruments
for putting up a house and pulling down.

SOLSTICES
From *Time and Ladbroke Square*

Ladbroke Square: one place
where I can be sure that
like a poultice of green
the heavy summer trees
the branches and leaves which veil
the houses, dim the traffic sounds
will always soothe me

– where, to absorb the fact
that a word can betray
a thesaurus of misunderstanding
I have paced the boundaries,
quartered every alternative
path, a peripatetic
who needs to think on her feet

– where I know I shall find
in the frozen lull between
solstice and full moon
though everything seems dead,
the first resistless push of buds
and almost colourless frills
of embryonic growth

one place where – and when:
whether at the year's nadir
its lowest gear before
the sky-wheel creeks forward
or its zenith of ripeness –
to learn about recurrence
and transformation.

THE TREES ARE DOWN

– and he cried with a loud voice:
Hurt not the earth, neither the sea, nor the trees –
(Revelation)

They are cutting down the great plane-trees at the
       end of the gardens.
For days there has been the grate of the saw, the swish
       of the branches as they fall,
The crash of the trunks, the rustle of trodden leaves,
With the 'Whoops' and the 'Whoas,' the loud
        common talk, the loud common laughs of
        the men, above it all.

I remember one evening of a long past Spring
Turning in at a gate, getting out of a cart, and finding
       a large dead rat in the mud of the drive.
I remember thinking: alive or dead, a rat was a god-
       forsaken thing,
But at least, in May, that even a rat should be alive.

The week's work here is as good as done. There is just
       one bough
  On the roped bole, in the fine grey rain,

Green and high
   And lonely against the sky.
      (Down now! –)
   And but for that,
   If an old dead rat
Did once, for a moment, unmake the Spring, I might
      never have thought of him again.

It is not for a moment the Spring is unmade to-day;
These were great trees, it was in them from root to
      stem:
When the men with the 'Whoops' and the 'Whoas'
      have carted the whole of the whispering
      loveliness away
Half the Spring, for me, will have gone with them.

It is going now, and my heart has been struck with
      the hearts of the planes;
Half my life it has beat with these, in the sun, in the
      rains,
   In the March wind, the May breeze,
In the great gales that came over to them across the
      roofs from the great seas.
   There was only a quiet rain when they were
      dying;
   They must have heard the sparrows flying,

And the small creeping creatures in the earth where
        they were lying –
    But I, all day, I heard an angel crying:
        'Hurt not the trees.'

EARTHQUAKE IN CAMDEN TOWN
From *Dombey and Son*

The first shock of a great earthquake had, just at that period, rent the whole neighbourhood to its centre. Traces of its course were visible on every side. Houses were knocked down; streets broken through and stopped; deep pits and trenches dug in the ground; enormous heaps of earth and clay thrown up; buildings that were undermined and shaking, propped by great beams of wood. Here, a chaos of carts, overthrown and jumbled together, lay topsy-turvy at the bottom of a steep unnatural hill; there, confused treasures of iron soaked and rusted in something that had accidentally become a pond. Everywhere were bridges that led nowhere; thoroughfares that were wholly impassable; Babel towers of chimneys, wanting half their height; temporary wooden houses and enclosures, in the most unlikely situations; carcases of ragged tenements, and fragments of unfinished walls and arches, and piles of scaffolding, and wildernesses of bricks, and giant forms of cranes, and tripods straddling above nothing. There were a hundred thousand shapes and substances of incompleteness, wildly mingled out of their places, upside down, burrowing in the earth, aspiring in the air, mouldering in the water, and unintelligible as any dream. Hot springs and fiery eruptions, the usual attendants upon earthquakes, lent their contributions of confusion to the scene. Boiling water hissed and heaved within dilapidated walls; whence, also, the glare and roar of flames came issuing forth; and mounds of ashes blocked up rights of way, and wholly changed the law and custom of the neighbourhood.

In short, the yet unfinished and unopened Railroad was in progress; and, from the very core of all this dire disorder, trailed smoothly away, upon its mighty course of civilisation and improvement.

LONDON

This London of cast-iron and bronze, my soul,
where under shed-roofs sheets of metal clang;
    where sailing ships disappear, without Notre Dame
for star, disappear, out there, towards fate.

Stations of soot and smoke, where the gas weeps
its spleens of distant silver towards paths of light
    where beasts of boredom yawn at the hour
that chimes, immensely mournful, from Westminster.

And this unending embankment of deadly lamps,
the fates whose spindles dive to the depths;
    and these drowned mariners, beneath petals
of mud flowers where the flame casts its glimmers.

And these gestures of drunken women and these
    shawls,
this liquor in golden letters high as roofs,
    and suddenly death amongst these multitudes,
O my evening soul, this dark London that drags in
    you.

226   EMILE VERHAEREN (1855–1916)
    TRANSLATED BY WILL STONE

From MILTON

From Golgonooza the spiritual Four-fold London
　　eternal,
In immense labours & sorrows, ever building, ever
　　falling,
Thro' Albion's four Forests which overspread all the
　　Earth
From London Stone to Blackheath east: to Hounslow
　　west:
To Finchley north: to Norwood south: and the
　　weights
Of Enitharmon's Loom play lulling cadences on the
　　winds of Albion
From Caithness in the north to Lizard-point & Dover
　　in the south.

Loud sounds the Hammer of Los & loud his Bellows
　　is heard
Before London to Hampstead's breadths and
　　Highgate's heights,
To Stratford & old Bow & across to the Gardens of
　　Kensington
On Tyburn's Brook: loud groans Thames beneath the
　　iron Forge
Of Rintrah & Palamabron, of Theotorm & Bromion,
　　to forge the instruments

Of Harvest, the Plow & Harrow to pass over the
     Nations.

The Surrey hills glow like the clinkers of the furnace;
     Lambeth's Vale
Where Jerusalem's foundations began, where they
     were laid in ruins,
Where they were laid in ruins from every Nation,
     & Oak Groves rooted,
Dark gleams before the Furnace-mouth a heap of
     burning ashes.
When shall Jerusalem return & overspread all the
     Nations?
Return, return to Lambeth's Vale, O building of
     human souls!
[. .]

IN THE FIRE-FROST MORNING

In the fire-frost morning the geese drive south
Trailing hosannas over the estuaries
And the beasts on the clockhouse stir.
From Tottenham Hale to Hackney Downs
The trumpets of day sound
And the gulls swarm up like heralds
Over the sleepers. Awake! Awake!
Throw open your skylights, thrust your heads to see:
Horseshoe thicket is afire with dawn
And the waters on Spring Hill teem.
Doors, dance. Fill the houses with praises.
God's promise blazes in the reedbeds,
Bursting over the winter willows and sallows
All the way down to waiting Walthamstow.

ON LIVING IN AN AREA OF MANIFEST GREYNESS AND MISERY

'London is a vast ocean in which survival is
not certain.'

'Essex Road and the unluckily named Balls Pond
Road are areas of manifest greyness and misery.'
Peter Ackroyd, *London: the Biography*

I sleep high on the bird's nest.
Trucks and lorries shake the house
and make the bricks tremble,
roaring tidal waves rock the bed
and put me to sleep.
There are odd wrecked Georgian houses
beached between tyre shops and takeaways.
Sometimes people are murdered.
Police sirens shriek up and down all day
like seagulls chasing sandwiches.
On the second floor,
we can look right into the 38
and see all the people
but we think they can't see us.
And we can jump on the 38 ourselves,
sail on the top deck
down to Bloomsbury and Victoria.

Our walls are stuffed with horsehair,
on stormy nights we hear the horses gallop.
Like us, they don't want to leave.
The ghost of a cat lives next door.
Young black drivers play hip-hop and dance hall,
when they stop it's a five-minute party
and you never know when it might happen.
The pink-haired squatters dance topless
on the concrete roof when it's hot.
John Ball's pond lies under our back gardens,
the shades of his cows low at full moon.
But it's the roll of traffic
that makes it more of an ocean
especially the sound of rushing wheels
when it rains,
and the uniformed Catholic children
slip along the wet pavement
like blue fish
swimming down the Balls Pond Road.

MARTINA EVANS (1961 –)   231

IF IT WASN'T FOR THE 'OUSES
IN BETWEEN

If you saw my little backyard,
'Wot a pretty spot,' you'd cry,
It's a picture on a sunny summer day;
Wiv the turnip tops and cabbages
Wot people doesn't buy,
I makes it on a Sunday look all gay.

The neighbours finks I grow 'em
And you'd fancy you're in Kent,
Or at Epsom if you gaze into the mews;
It's a wonder as the landlord
Doesn't want to raise the rent,
Because we have such nobby distant views.

Oh! it really is a wery pretty garden
And Chingford to the Eastward could be seen;
Wiv a ladder and some glasses
You could see to 'Ackney Marshes
If it wasn't for the 'ouses in between.

We're as countrified as can be
Wiv a clothes prop for a tree;
The tub-stool makes a rustic little stile;
Ev'ry time the blooming clock strikes

There's a cuckoo sings to me
And I've painted up 'To Leather Lane A Mile'.

Wiv tomatoes and wiv radishes
Wot 'adn't any sale,
The backyard looks a purfick mass o' bloom,
And I've made a little beehive
Wiv some beetles in a pail
And a pitchfork wiv the 'andle of a broom.

Oh! it really is a wery pretty garden
And Rye 'Ouse from the cock-loft could be seen,
Where the chickweed man undresses
To bathe 'mong the water cresses,
If it wasn't for the 'ouses in between.

There's the bunny shares his egg box
Wiv the cross-eyed cock and hen,
Though they 'as got the pip and him the 'morf;
In a dog's 'ouse on the line-post
There was pigeons, nine or ten,
Till someone took a brick and knocked it off.

The dust cart though it seldom comes
Is just like 'Arvest 'Ome
And we made to rig a dairy up some'ow;
Put the donkey in the wash'ouse

Wiv some imitation 'orns,
For we're teaching im to moo just like a kah.

Oh! it really is a wery pretty garden
And 'Endon to the westward could be seen,
And by clinging to the chimbley
You could see across to Wembley,
If it wasn't for the 'ouses in between.

Though the gasworks is at Woolwich
They improve the rural scene,
For mountains they would very nicely pass;
There's the mushrooms in the dust-hole
With the cowcumbers so green
It only wants a bit o' 'ouse glass.

I wears this milkman's nightshirt
And I sits outside all day
Like the ploughboy cove what's mizzled o'er the Lea;
And when I goes indoors at night
They dunno what I say,
'Cause my language gets as yokel as can be.

Oh! it really is a wery pretty garden
And soapworks from the 'ousetops could be seen;
If I got a rope and pulley
I'd enjoy the breeze more fully,
If it wasn't for the 'ouses in between.

234   EDGAR BATEMAN (1860–1946)

From FOX RUNNING

Fox
running
loose in his sleek skin
loose in his slick fur

Fox
between lamp dark and daylight
loping through the suburbs
miles bridges canals rails

Through the town littorals
chicken runs long bricked over
wild places put to the plough

Streets keeping their tilt
and curve of old lanes
over Crouch Hill into Seven Sisters

Through Haringey Hornsey
Highgate Holloway the cold
wind of the subway tunnels

Out under the sky Highbury
Hampstead to Paddington
among the grey yellow bricks

Chimneys and flat house fronts
his London skyline, pencil
of the Post Office Tower
his marker for Baker Street

Along the bottom line
of Regent's Park for Camden
hiding out along the waterway

Fox
ranging the city's inner spaces
being scavenger of skips parks
and desirable period residences

Fox wanting to be alongwind
amongst bracken his own shade
the breeze at his back

One eye sleeping, shut
on some chicken dream of wire
and bloody feathers in his nostrils

One eye awake to his hunters
and the slavering jaws
of the hunting dogs, his brothers once

Being outlaw
out classed out priced out manoeuvred
hunger leashing him in to the city
in the rattling milk bottle dawn

Back of his mind brome blowing
wind sifting the oak leaves
back of a stone littered silence

Back of his fox skull
mountain ash and the wide sky
printing his memory's tape

In at last from the wide
improbable country the townsmen
gape at uncertain such space
ever was for running: the fox

Aloof distant alert
holed up between running
in his red slash of fox body
running from the emptied distance

Crowded with townspill
of building sites' muddy footings
where will be flyover
industrial estate new bungalows

Years ago long ago late he is
skin of his name of his legend
skin of his alias son of his alibi
son of his tale told for children

Running into the tube maps
into the bus routes into the rails
learning the districts
learning connections and running

Into the city
dawn glimpsed and sometime sighted
I've seen him running
from Lancaster Gate to the Long Water

Poor winded breath shortening
and his thatch thins, wanderer

Running into his death
and his death always with him

Running into the razor
heart attack up his sleeve
shotgun pepper in his backside
[·]

From JERUSALEM

The fields from Islington to Marybone,
To Primrose Hill and Saint John's Wood,
   Were builded over with pillars of gold,
And there Jerusalem's pillars stood.

   Her Little-ones ran on the fields,
The Lamb of God among them seen,
   And fair Jerusalem his Bride,
Among the little meadows green.

   Pancrass & Kentish-town repose
Among her golden pillars high,
   Among her golden arches which
Shine upon the starry sky.

   The Jew's-harp-house & the Green Man,
The Ponds where Boys to bathe delight,
   The fields of Cows by Willan's farm,
Shine in Jerusalem's pleasant sight.

   She walks upon our meadows green,
The Lamb of God walks by her side,
   And every English Child is seen
Children of Jesus & his Bride.

Forgiving trespasses and sins
Lest Babylon with cruel Og
   With Moral & Self-righteous Law
Should crucify in Satan's Synagogue!

   What are these golden Builders doing
Near mournful ever-weeping Paddington,
   Standing above that mighty Ruin
Where Satan the first victory won,

   Where Albion slept beneath the Fatal Tree,
And the Druids' golden Knife
   Rioted in human gore,
In Offerings of Human Life?

   They groan'd aloud on London Stone,
They groan'd aloud on Tyburn's Brook,
   Albion gave his deadly groan,
And all the Atlantic Mountains shook.

   Albion's Spectre from his Loins
Tore forth in all the pomp of War:
   Satan his name: in flames of fire
He stretch'd his Druid Pillars far.

Jerusalem fell from Lambeth's Vale
Down thro' Poplar & Old Bow,
   Thro' Malden and acros the Sea,
In War & Howling, death & woe.

[·]

THE REVERIE OF POOR SUSAN

At the corner of Wood Street, when daylight appears,
Hangs a Thrush that sings loud, it has sung for three
    years:
Poor Susan has passed by the spot, and has heard
In the silence of morning the song of the Bird.

'Tis a note of enchantment; what ails her? She sees
A mountain ascending, a vision of trees;
Bright volumes of vapour through Lothbury glide,
And a river flows on through the vale of Cheapside.

Green pastures she views in the midst of the dale,
Down which she so often has tripped with her pail;
And a single small cottage, a nest like a dove's,
The one only dwelling on earth that she loves.

She looks, and her heart is in heaven: but they fade,
The mist and the river, the hill and the shade:
The stream will not flow, and the hill will not rise,
And the colours have all passed away from her eyes!

SEVEN DIALS, LONDON, 1880
From *Lara*

The sweaty armpit of London: the seven septic
streets of sore-raddled Seven Dials welcomed

the Robbins' family into its flea-infested embrace:
a windowless dungeon in a collapsing tenement

in a yard without water or sunlight at the end
of an alley running slimy with effluence.

This was where the newly-arrived washed up –
green-eyed, open-mouthed, desperate, forced

to cohabit with robbers, ruffians, rouged harlots,
to endure the torture of endlessly clattering carts,

grating knife-grinders, beggars, dog-breakers,
parrot-sellers, herring-hawkers, metal-workers,

of brawling drunks and bawling women in labour.
Oh, how they suffered in summer's grease-slathered

mugginess, its toothless, foul-mouthed breath,
particles of coal dust coating once-healthy lungs.

Never again the evensong of nightingales in the
   woods,
Never again the percussive clatter of rain on the
   Camcor.
Never again the crisp, clean oxygen of home –
   Ireland.

KERR'S ASS

We borrowed the loan of Kerr's ass
To go to Dundalk with butter,
Brought him home the evening before the market
And exile that night in Mucker.

We heeled up the cart before the door,
We took the harness inside –
The straw-stuffed straddle, the broken breeching
With bits of bull-wire tied;

The winkers that had no choke-band,
The collar and the reins . . .
In Ealing Broadway, London Town
I name their several names

Until a world comes to life –
Morning, the silent bog,
And the God of imagination waking
In a Mucker fog.

PATRICK KAVANAGH (1904–67)

SOME LONDONERS

ALL SPECIMENS OF MAN
From *The Prelude: Book VII*

Now homeward through the thickening hubbub,
    where
See, among less distinguishable shapes,
The Italian, with his Frame of Images
Upon his head; with Basket at his waist
The Jew; the stately and slow-moving Turk
With freight of slippers piled beneath his arm.
Briefly, we find, if tired of random sights
And haply to that search our thoughts should turn,
Among the crowd, conspicuous less or more,
As we proceed, all specimens of man
Through all the colours which the sun bestows,
And every character of form and face,
The Swede, the Russian; from the genial South,
The Frenchman and the Spaniard, from remote
America, the Hunter-Indian; the Moors,
Malays, Lascars, the Tartars and Chinese,
And Negro Ladies in white muslin gowns.

WHITECHAPEL IN BRITAIN

Pumbedita, Cordova, Cracow, Amsterdam,
Vilna, Lublin, Berditchev and Volozhin,
Your names will always be sacred,
Places where Jews have been.

And sacred is Whitechapel,
It is numbered with our Jewish towns.
Holy, holy, holy
Are your bombed stones.

If we ever have to leave Whitechapel,
As other Jewish towns were left,
Its soul will remain a part of us,
Woven into us, woof and weft.

A LONG LOOK BACK

London's my town and proud of it
I am, though born in a street of it
more like a ditch,
with a smell like a Polish Baghdad
that bothered the rich.

Me, I was one of a big quarrelsome family.
We could swear in lots of languages
and thought grass
was something delicate, very uncommon,
a rare place

To make love in a shut park
but not to dance on even in the dark;
sort of a paradise,
gates open to let you out and closed to keep you out
sunset to sunrise.

Something was always happening in our street.
We had a genuine witch, Chaya,
and a black-eyed rascal, Meyer.
Chaya hadn't a crust
but could stop babies;
Meyer gambled and got bust
but made babies.

We even had a murder once
when Yossel, the tailor,
stabbed his missus's sailor
with a scissors.
But mostly the only thing that got murdered
was English,
and the only thing that got in the papers
was fish.

It's all different now, like after a revolution.
You don't have a wash there, but an ablution,
if you don't mind!
You can even walk on the grass anytime,
and the gates are gone
like any respectable place in London.

Chaya, poor witch, dead,
they say. Meyer married.
The old faces all gone, only
sometimes a ghost shuffling by,
talking to the wind and lonely.

THE MOUNTAINS O' MOURNE

Oh, Mary, this London's a wonderful sight,
With people all working by day and by night.
Sure, they don't sow potatoes, nor barley, nor wheat,
But there's gangs of them digging for gold in
    the street.
At least when I asked them that's what I was told,
So I just took a hand at this digging for gold,
But for all that I found there I might as well be
Where the Mountains o' Mourne sweep down to
    the sea.

I believe that when writing a wish you expressed
As to how the fine ladies in London are dressed,
Well if you'll believe me, when asked to a ball,
They don't wear no top to their dresses at all.
Oh I've seen them meself and you could not in truth,
Say if they were bound for a ball or a bath.
Don't be starting such fashions, now, Mary, *mo chroí*,
Where the Mountains o' Mourne sweep down to
    the sea.

I've seen England's king from the top of a bus
And I've never known him, but he means to know us.
And tho' by the Saxon we once were oppressed,
Still I cheered, God forgive me, I cheered with the rest.
And now that he's visited Erin's green shore
We'll be much better friends than we've been
        heretofore
When we've got all we want, we're as quiet as can be
Where the Mountains o' Mourne sweep down to
        the sea.

You remember young Peter O'Loughlin, of course,
Well, now he is here at the head of the Force.
I met him today, I was crossing the Strand,
And he stopped the whole street with a wave of his
        hand.
And there we stood talkin' of days that are gone,
While the whole population of London looked on.
But for all these great powers he's wishful like me,
To be back where the dark Mournes sweep down to
        the sea.

There's beautiful girls here, oh, never you mind,
With beautiful shapes nature never designed,
And lovely complexions all roses and cream,
But let me remark with regard to the same
That if of those roses you ventured to sip,
The colours might all come away on your lip,
So I'll wait for the wild rose that's waiting for me
In the place where the dark Mournes sweep down to
    the sea.

PERCY FRENCH (1854–1920)

GRAND UNION BRIDGE

I'd take this bridge over the Paddington Cut
for Saturday Morning Pictures at the cinema
where Riley shot Dixon in *The Blue Lamp*.

Irish name, like his sidekick 'Spud' Murphy,
like this canal's cutters, like my own family's,
over for work, songless in a strange land.

In class I was asked *Is it called Paddington
because of all the Paddys who live there?*
My brother changed his name from Paddy.

A duckweed green screen on the Cut today
clothes this song so it can slip mermaid-like
into the Land of the Young, an otherworld

where human visitors will never grow old,
unless they touch the land of home again.
I remember a young Irish girl landed here:

winter's black glass skin screened the Cut;
a copper sold reporters her note for drink.
We all read it in *The Paddington Mercury*;

the girl was told a fairy story: words hollow
as his rolled gold ring: rolled over, she rolled
in cold canal water, an iceberg of tears, melting.

If you want to know the time ask a policeman,
runs the old song; he'll know it's all relative,
how it can be a stretch, or suspended, like a

sentence or Riley dancing the Paddington Jig.
But Dixon rose again to star in his own show,
black and white as its plots, thin as a film strip

or ribbon round an empty wedding box. Cut.

LONDON IS THE PLACE FOR ME

London is the place for me
London this lovely city
You can go to France or America,
India, Asia or Australia
But you must come back to London city
Well believe me I am speaking broadmindedly
I am glad to know my Mother Country
I have been travelling to countries years ago
But this is the place I wanted to know
London that is the place for me

To live in London you are really comfortable
Because the English people are very much sociable
They take you here and they take you there
And they make you feel like a millionaire
London that's the place for me

At night when you have nothing to do
You can take a walk down Shaftesbury Avenue
There you will laugh and talk and enjoy the breeze
And admire the beautiful scenery
Of London that's the place for me

Yes, I cannot complain of the time I have spent
I mean my life in London is really magnificent
I have every comfort and every sport
And my residence is Hampton Court
So London, that's the place for me

ALDWYN ROBERTS (LORD KITCHENER)
(1922–2000)

INGLAN IS A BITCH

wen mi jus come to Landan toun
mi use to work pan di andahgroun
but workin pan di andahgroun
yu dont get fi know your way aroun

Inglan is a bitch
dere's no escapin it
Inglan is a bitch
dere's no runin whe fram it

mi get a likkle jab in a big otell
an awftah a while, mi woz doin quite well
dem staat mi awf as a dish-washah
but wen mi tek a stack, mi noh tun clack-watchah!

Inglan is a bitch
dere's no escapin it
Inglan is a bitch
noh baddah try fi hide fram it

wen dem gi you di likkle wage packit
fus dem rab it wid dem big tax rackit
yu haffi struggle fi mek enz meet
an wen yu goh a yu bed yu jus cant sleep

Inglan is a bitch
dere's no escapin it
Inglan is a bitch fi true
a noh lie mi a tell, a true

mi use to work dig ditch wen it cowl noh bitch
mi did strang like a mule, but, bwoy, mi did fool
den awftah a while mi jus stap dhu owevahtime
den awftah a while mi jus phu dung mi tool

Inglan is a bitch
dere's no escapin it
Inglan is a bitch
yu haffi know how fi suvive in it

well mi dhu day wok an mi dhu nite wok
mi dhu clean wok an mi dhu dutty wok
dem seh dat black man is very lazy
but if yu si how mi wok yu woodah seh mi crazy

Inglan is a bitch
dere's no escapin it
Inglan is a bitch
yu bettah face up to it

dem have a likkle facktri up inna Brackly
inna disya facktri all dem dhu is pack crackry

fi di laas fifteen years dem get mi laybah
now awftah fifteen years mi fall out a fayvah

Inglan is a bitch
dere's no escapin it
Inglan is a bitch
dere's no runnin whe fram it

mi know dem have wok, wok in abundant
yet still, dem mek mi redundant
now, at fifty-five mi getin quite ole
yet still, dem sen mi fi goh draw dole

Inglan is a bitch
dere's no escapin it
Inglan is a bitch fi true
is whe wi a goh dhu bout it?

IMMIGRANT

November '63: eight months in London.
I pause on the low bridge to watch the pelicans:
they float swanlike, arching their white necks
over only slightly ruffled bundles of wings,
burying awkward beaks in the lake's water.

I clench cold fists in my Marks and Spencer's jacket
and secretly test my accent once again:
St. James's Park; St. James's Park; St. James's Park.

WHAT AILS THE KING?

*He who drinks a tumbler of London water has literally
in his stomach more animated beings than there are
men and women and children on the face of the earth.*
REVEREND SYDNEY SMITH 1771–1845

A tumbler of London water
A tumbler of London water
And make that sparkling hybrid.
A King can't have enough of this multi-fluid.

I want to feel as Druid as oak
as Roman as Severus, that Libyan bloke,
as pagan-powered as up-in-arms Boadicea
as lettered as that black Victorian Sancho.

O water from the well of hidden histories
as angel-fruitful as Blake's Peckham Rye tree
as Sabbath-lit as a Jewish window
as spice-warm as a Huguenot-haunted curry house.

I want to salaam as shalom
and be dragon-driven as Chinatown
where old grey Thames meets the Yellow River
and the little bardic people of the Irish Sea.

My kingdom, I say, my sceptered kingdom
for a tumbler of London H_2O.
Let animated beings invade my being.
Let a King imbibe the globe in one swallow.

SIR TOPAZ & DA ELEPHANT
From *Telling Tales*

I be
    Sir Topaz, E3 bling king
    so dazzling you be blinking
    pack punches till they sink in
    I be Twitter, you be LinkedIn
    online the girls I reel in
    it's pep-talk that I deal in
    but Pepsi's not the real thing
    ask your homegirl how she feeling

(applause)

> *Da Elephant, I'm eloquent,*
> *the heavyweight of grime,*
> *me rhymes are sick, I'm gonna pick*
> *your pocket full of rhyme,*
> *South London's king, so I'm linked in,*
> *you're out to lunch on bhang,*
> *like David slew Goliath, you*
> *will slay yourself with slang*

(applause)

You be

    so slow you slump on the bassline
    I jump off the beat, don't waste time
    hundred kilos, watch your waistline,
    I tasted your girl, she taste fine
    I'm hungry, speaking of lunchtime
    I burn up cals on the frontline
    your trunk's defunct, her cunt's mine,
    you be out for 9 on that punchline

(mad applause and booing)

    You double dealt below the belt
    but I will bust your screen,
    you shoot your load in virtual mode
    cos you're a fairy queen,
    you stole my girl, she said you smell
    your dick's a Bic, a biro,
    you write your rhymes and learn your lines
    and gamble all your giro

(mad applause and booing)

You be

    breaking up in your nearly new style
    mess with me but you know it's futile
    I got your girl, she's nubile,

you got three heads, look at you, vile,
one says I'm gay but you retrial
one says I shafted your female
one says fuck-all cos it's penile!
Stick that up your trunk for a freestyle!

(mad applause)

> *You got no creds, I got three heads,*
> *they're body, mind and soul*
> *but dickhead, you have only one*
> *that's why you're on the dole*

(applause)

I be
    Sir Topaz, claiming my last dole
    just signed a deal in charcoal
    not a fat cat sitting on me arsehole,
    shoot rhymes from a metaphor arsenal,
    one step ahead, metatarsal,
    up there with Wiley & Rascal,
    you be doggerel, I'm artful,
    Elephant, fuck off back to your Castle . . .

(mad applause . . .)

THE MAUNDER'S PRAISE OF HIS STROWLING MORT

Doxy oh! thy Glaziers shine
As glimmar by the Salomon,
No Gentry Mort hath prats like thine,
No Cove e'er wap'd with such a one.

White thy fambles, red thy gan,
And thy quarrons dainty is,
Couch a hogshead with me than,
In the Darkmans clip and kiss.

What though I no Togeman wear,
Nor Commission, Mish, or slate,
Store of strummel wee'l have here
And i' th' Skipper lib in state.

Wapping thou I know dost love,
Else the Ruffin cly the Mort,
From thy stampers then remove
Thy Drawers, and let's prig in sport.

When the Lightmans up do's call
Margery Prater from her nest,
And her Cackling cheats withal,
In a Boozing Ken wee'l feast.

There if Lour we want I'l mill
A Gage or nip for thee a bung,
Rum booz thou shalt booz thy fill
And crash a Grunting cheat that's young.

Bing awast to Rome-vile then,
O my dimber wapping Dell;
Wee'l have a booth and dock agen,
Then trining scape and all is well.

NIGHT'S SCAVENGERS

These scavengers for wood beside the Thames,
I take in their glutinous, brown, tar-like stink.
In the sieve of their thick, matted hair,
They trap all the dirt and the darkness of London.
Their exile shelters, nurtures them in silence.
I too am a scavenger,
I too am an exile,
Looking to join them,
Born again,
A scavenger of words beside the Thames.
But their exile is deeper than mine.
I see their make-shift shelters from the rain –
Boxes, slumped against concrete walls –
And how they coil inside,
Intoxicated spirits,
Eyelids heavy with numbness.
For warmth, I squat in a phone booth, staring out.
A sparrow of ice alights.
A woman's lips leave a promise on the glass.
My palm throbs between cheek and pillow.
The smell of weaning plugs my nostrils.
I hear the gentle swish-swish of autumn foliage.
A train on some nearby platform sighs.
A suitcase hesitates to move.

FAWZI KARIM (1945–2019)   271
TRANSLATED BY ANTHONY HOWELL
AND ABBAS KADHIM

'WHY SHOULD I CARE FOR THE MEN OF THAMES'

Why should I care for the men of Thames,
Or the cheating waves of charter'd streams,
Or shrink at the little blasts of fear
That the hireling blows into my ear?

Tho' born on the cheating banks of Thames,
Tho' his waters bathed my infant limbs,
The Ohio shall wash his stains from me:
I was born a slave, but I go to be free.

DIRECTIONS
after Billy Collins

You know the wild bush at the back of the flat,
the one that scrapes the kitchen window,
the one that struggles for soil and water
and fails where the train tracks scar the ground?
And you know how if you leave the bush
and walk the stunted land, you come
to crossroads, paved just weeks ago:
hot tar over the flattened roots of trees,
and a squad of traffic lights, red-eyed now
stiff against the filth-stained fallen leaves?

And farther on, you know
the bruised allotments with the broken sheds
and if you go beyond that you hit
the first block of Thomas Street Estate?
Well, if you enter and ascend, and you
might need a running jump over
dank puddles into the shaking lift
that goes no further than the fourth floor,
you will eventually come to a rough rise
of stairs that reach without railings
the run-down roof as high as you can go
and a good place to stop.

The best time is late evening
when the moon fights through
drifts of fumes as you are walking,
and when you find an upturned bin
to sit on, you will be able to see
the smog pour across the city
and blur the shapes and tones
of things and you will be attacked
by the symphony of tyres, airplanes,
sirens, screams, engines –
and if this is your day you might even
catch a car chase or hear a horde
of biker boys thunder-cross a bridge.

But it is tough to speak of these things,
how tufts of smog enter the body
and begin to wind us down,
how the city chokes us painfully against
its chest made of secrets and fire,
how we, built of weaker things, regard
our sculpted landscape, water flowing
through pipes, the clicks of satellites
passing over clouds and the roofs
where we stand in the shudder of progress
giving ourselves to the vast outsides.

Still, text me before you set out.
Knock when you reach my door
and I will walk you as far as the tracks
with water for your travels and a hug.
I will watch after you and not turn back
to the flat till you merge
with the throngs of buses and cyclists –
heading down toward the block,
scuffing the ground with your feet.

ACKNOWLEDGMENTS

Thanks are due to the following copyright holders for permission to reprint:

FLEUR ADCOCK: 'Immigrant' from *Poems 1960–2000* (Bloodaxe Books, 2000). Reproduced with permission of Bloodaxe Books. www.bloodaxebooks.com JOHN AGARD: 'What Ails the King?' from *Travel Light Travel Dark* (Bloodaxe Books, 2013). Reproduced with permission of Bloodaxe Books. www.bloodaxebooks.com PATIENCE AGBABI: 'Sir Topaz & Da Elephant' from *Telling Tales*, Canongate Books, 2014. FERGUS ALLEN: 'Imperial War Museum, November' from *Who Goes There?* (Faber & Faber Limited, 1996). SAMUEL BECKETT: 'Serena I' from *The Collected Poems of Samuel Beckett* (Faber & Faber Limited, 2012). Reprinted with permission. Excerpt from *The Collected Poems of Samuel Beckett* by Samuel Beckett, copyright © 1930, 1935, 1961, 1977, 1989 by Samuel Beckett. Copyright © 2012 by the Estate of Samuel Beckett. Copyright © 1978, 1992 by Samuel Beckett/Editions de Minuit. Used by permission of Grove/Atlantic, Inc. Any third party use of this material, outside of this publication, is prohibited. JOHN BETJEMAN: 'Business Girls' and 'On Seeing an Old Poet in the Café Royal' from *Collected Poems* (1989), John Murray Press, an imprint of Hodder and Stoughton Limited. © The Estate of John Betjeman 1955, 1958, 1960, 1962, 1964, 1966, 1970, 1979, 1980, 1981, 2001. Introduction Andrew Motion © 2006. Reproduced by permission of John Murray Press, an imprint of Hodder and Stoughton Limited, and 37 lines from *Summoned by Bells*, John Murray Press, an imprint of Hodder and Stoughton Limited. © The Estate of John Betjeman 1955, 1958, 1960, 1962, 1964, 1966, 1970, 1979, 1980, 1981, 2001. Introduction Griff Rhys Jones. Reproduced by permission of John Murray Press, an imprint of Hodder and Stoughton Limited. PETER BOSTOCK: 'A Few Words from Rev. Sydney Smith' from *All that Glisters* (2008). Reprinted with kind permission from Ann Bostock. JOYCE CARY: Extract from *The Horse's Mouth*. Andrew Lownie Literary Agency. TOM CHIVERS: 'The Bells' from *Dark Islands*, Test Centre Publications, 2015. © Prototype. Reprinted with permission of the poet. HILARY DAVIES: 'In the Fire-frost Morning' from *Exile and the Kingdom*. Reprinted with permission from Enitharmon Press. IAN DUHIG: 'Grand Union Bridge' from forthcoming *Selected Poems*, Picador UK/Pan Macmillan. LAWRENCE DURRELL: 'A Ballad of the Good Lord Nelson' from *Collected Poems 1931–1974* (Faber & Faber Limited, 1980). Reprinted with permission. Curtis Brown UK. T. S. ELIOT: 2 extracts: (i) 26 lines from 'The river's tent is broken . . .' (ii) 9 lines from 'Unreal city . . .' from *The Waste Land* by T. S. Eliot. Reprinted with permission from Faber & Faber Limited. INUA ELLAMS: 'Directions' from *Candy Coated Unicorns and Converse All Stars* by Inua Ellams. Published by Flipped Eye, 2011. Copyright © Inua Ellams. Reproduced by permission of the author c/o Rogers, Coleridge & White Ltd, 20 Powis Mews, London W11 1JN. WILLIAM EMPSON: 'Homage to the British Museum' from *The Complete Poems* (Penguin UK, 2001). Reproduced with permission of Curtis Brown Ltd, London, on behalf of the Estate of William Empson. Copyright 2001 © William Empson. MARTINA EVANS: 'On Living in an Area of Manifest Greyness and Misery' from *The Windows of Graceland: New and Selected Poems*. Reprinted with permission from Carcanet Press. BERNARDINE EVARISTO: 'Seven Dials, London, 1880' from *Lara* (Bloodaxe Books, 2009). Reproduced with permission of Bloodaxe Books. www.bloodaxebooks.com RUTH FAINLIGHT: 'Solstice' from *Ruth Fainlight: New & Collected Poems* (Bloodaxe Books, 2010). Reproduced with permission of Bloodaxe Books. www.bloodaxebooks.com U. A. FANTHORPE: 'Rising Damp' and 'Portraits of Tudor Statesmen' from *Beginner's Luck* (Bloodaxe Books, 2019). Reproduced with permission of Bloodaxe Books. www.bloodaxebooks.com THOM GUNN: 'Keats at Highgate' from *Collected Poems*. Reprinted with permission from Faber & Faber

& Faber), reproduced by permission of David Higham Associates. DEREK MAHON: 'One of These Nights'. By kind permission of the Estate of Derek Mahon and The Gallery Press, Loughcrew, Oldcastle, County Meath, Ireland, from *The Poems (1961–2020)* (2021). ERIC MASCHWITZ: 'A Nightingale Sang in Berkeley Square'. Reprinted with the kind permission of Eric Maschwitz Musicals Limited. GEOFFREY MATTHEWS: 'Aubade 1940' from *War Poems* by Geoffrey Matthews, ed. Arnold Rattenbury, Whiteknights Press, Reading, 1989. IAN NAIRN: 'St. Stephen Walbrook' and 'Red Lion, Duke of York Street' from *Nairn's London* (Penguin, 1966). SYLVIA PLATH: 'Queen Mary's Rose Garden' from *Collected Poems* (Faber & Faber Limited, 1981). Reprinted with permission. 'Queen Mary's Rose Garden' from *The Collected Poems* by Sylvia Plath. Copyright © 1960, 1965, 1971, 1981 by the Estate of Sylvia Plath. Editorial material copyright © 1981 by Ted Hughes. Used by permission of HarperCollins Publishers. EZRA POUND: 'The Garden' from *Selected Poems*. Reprinted with permission from Faber & Faber Limited. 'The Garden' by Ezra Pound, from *Personae*, copyright ©1926 by Ezra Pound. Reprinted by permission of New Directions Publishing Corp. OLIVER REYNOLDS: 'Little Ease' from *Skevington's Daughter* (Faber & Faber Limited, 1985). Reprinted with permission. DENISE RILEY: 'Composed Beneath Westminster Bridge' from *Say Something Back* (Pan Macmillan, 2016). ARTHUR RIMBAUD (tr. OLIVER BERNARD): Extract from 'Villes' from *The Poems*, tr. Oliver Bernard, Anvil Press Poetry, 2012. Reprinted by kind permission of Carcanet Press, Manchester, UK. ALDWYN ROBERTS: 'London is the Place For Me' (1948). IMOGEN ROBERTSON: 'The Statues of Buckingham Palace' included in *City State: New London Poetry* (Penned in the Margins, 2009). Copyright © Imogen Robertson. Reprinted with permission from the poet. RICHARD SCOTT: 'Soho' (section ix) from *Soho* by Richard Scott. Copyright © 2018. Published by Faber & Faber Limited. Reprinted with permission. JO SHAPCOTT: '"Delectable

TITLES IN EVERYMAN'S LIBRARY
POCKET POETS